THE

FENG SHUI

KIT

風水

THE FENG SHUI KIT

The Chinese Way to Health, Wealth
and Happiness, at Home and at Work

Man-Ho Kwok
with Joanne O'Brien

Charles E. Tuttle Co., Inc.
Boston • Rutland, Vermont • Tokyo

First published in the United States in 1995 by
Charles E. Tuttle Company, Inc. of Rutland, Vermont and Tokyo, Japan,
with editorial offices at 153 Milk Street, Boston, Massachusetts 02109.

ISBN 0-8048-3047-9

7 9 10 8

AN EDDISON•SADD EDITION
Edited, designed and produced by
Eddison Sadd Editions Limited
St Chad's House, 148 King's Cross Road
London WC1X 9DH

Phototypeset in Berkeley and Baker Signet using QuarkXPress on Apple Macintosh
Origination by SX Composing, Raleigh, Essex
Produced by Mandarin Offset, printed and bound in Hong Kong

CONTENTS

P'an Ku, afraid that chaos would overwhelm the world, kept the sky and the earth apart for thousands of years before finally letting go when he was sure the world was safe.

THE CREATION OF P'AN KU

**The creation of the world and its many shapes and elements,
so vital to feng shui, is captured in the story of P'an Ku.
As a result of his personal sacrifice,
P'an Ku brought order to chaos and so gave birth to all life.**

Before time began there was an egg of inconceivable size. Darkness and chaos filled the egg, and out of the chaos P'an Ku was created. Nurtured by the darkness, he slowly developed and grew and for eighteen thousand years he was unaware of any life beyond the egg.

One day he was awoken by a sudden, sharp movement but he could not see anything through the darkness. At first he was fearful but his fear was replaced by anger at being trapped. He lashed out with his fists and shattered the hard black shell of the egg.

Darkness poured out of the egg, but so did the light that had been obscured for thousands of years. Everything that was clear and bright rose to the sky and everything that was muddy and heavy fell to the earth. For a long time the sky and the earth were clearly divided. But P'an Ku was afraid that the brightness above would fall onto the darkness below, and so he held the heavens aloft with his hands and kept the earth steady with his feet.

The years passed by, the sky and earth moved further apart but P'an Ku did not rest. Another eighteen thousand years passed and the earth and sky were so far apart that they could no longer be seen. But still P'an Ku would not let go in case chaos came pouring back. A further ten thousand years passed and at last P'an Ku was sure that the world was safe. He finally let go, but as he bowed his head he collapsed from exhaustion and began to die.

He let out one final breath which became the wind and the clouds, his deep voice rose as thunder, his left eye flew to the heavens to become the sun, and his right eye soon followed to become the moon. The lifeless body of P'an Ku fell to the earth; his limbs and torso became plains, hills and mountains, and his blood coursed through the earth filling rivers and lakes. His muscles were transformed into the soil and his tendons turned into paths and roads. His thick grey hair and long beard rose to become the stars, and his fine body hair and skin sank into the earth and took root as grass, trees and flowers. His bones, teeth and marrow changed into glistening rubies, jade and minerals.

P'an Ku had offered himself to the world, and by doing so gave birth to all life.

(Adapted from *Chinese Myths and Legends*, translated by Man-Ho Kwok, edited by Joanne O'Brien)

Wind

风

水

Water

CHAPTER ONE

WHAT IS FENG SHUI?

Have you ever walked into a strange house and immediately felt at home or sat in a garden where everything seems to be at peace? Or perhaps you have entered a room at home and felt uneasy but cannot explain why? What may appear to be a mystery to us can be explained through the art of *feng shui* (pronounced 'fung shway'), the ancient Chinese system of creating harmonious surroundings which bring happiness, prosperity and good health. The forces of the earth and the heavens may be balanced in one location but in turmoil in another. Without realizing, you may have blocked the smooth flow of *ch'i*, the life-giving energy the Chinese believe flows through our bodies and our surroundings, by the unfortunate positioning of a table or bed. Or perhaps a tree is too close to your house or the garden fence is too high. A professional feng shui master* would soon identify the source of your worries and offer you suggestions for change. But feng shui is more than a matter of understanding your local surroundings and thereby improving your fortune.

*Note: The art of feng shui was traditionally practised by males, hence the term feng shui 'master'. Today, although the professional expert is often male, feng shui can be practised with equal success by both men and women.

At one extreme, it is a way of interpreting the hidden and mysterious forces of the cosmos, and at the other, it is a practical approach to environmental planning. More than two thousand years ago, the Chinese were aware of the need to preserve the landscape, not just for aesthetic reasons but in the name of conservation. This plea to stop intensive grazing was written by the sage Mencius in the fourth century BC:

The trees on Ox mountain were once beautiful. However, because the mountain is on the borders of a great state, they were cut down with axes and saws, so how could they retain their beauty? Yet they continued through the cycle of life and the feeding of the rain and dew to put forth buds and new leaves. But the cattle and goats came and browsed amongst the trees and destroyed them. This is why the mountain is now bare and stripped. People look at it and think this is how it has always been. But this is not the true nature of the mountain. And this is also the case with humanity. Surely we were not without benevolence and righteousness? The way in which a person loses their true goodness is just like the way that trees are destroyed by the axe. Cut down day after day, how can the mind, anymore than the tree, retain its beauty or continue to live?

(*Mencius*, translated by D. C. Lau)

At the heart of feng shui is the desire to acknowledge the power of the natural world and to live in harmony with it. The characters literally mean wind/water and refer to the dynamic shaping effect of these elements upon our landscape. Feng shui also represents the power of the natural environment, which is alive with hidden forces. Those who put their trust in feng shui would say that you ignore or destroy natural features at your own peril. By clashing with the natural order, the Tao, you disturb the balance of yin and yang, the two fundamental forces of the universe. The process by which yin and yang are generated is captured in the following description, in which the Tao is referred to as the Great Ultimate, written by the Confucian philosopher Chou Tun-yi in the eleventh century AD:

The Great Ultimate through movement generates yang. When its activity reaches its limit, it becomes tranquil. Through tranquillity the Great Ultimate generates the yin. When tranquillity reaches its limit, activity begins again. Thus movement and tranquillity alternate and become the root of each other, giving rise to the distinction of yin and yang, and these two modes are thus established. By the transformation of yang and its union with yin, the five agents of water, fire, wood, metal and earth arise. When these five material forces (ch'i) are distributed in harmonious order, the four seasons run their course.

(*T'ai-chi't'u Shou, Sources of Chinese Tradition*, edited by Theodore de Bary)

The Chinese believe there is a dynamic interaction between these two forces which creates and sustains all life. Yin is feminine, cool and watery; it is the force in the moon, air and water. Yang is masculine, heavy and hot; it is the force in the earth and the sun, in thunder and in fire. Yin and yang exist in everything in different proportions that are continually changing.

The natural interaction of yin and yang should also be maintained on a personal level. Our nature and health reflect the movement of yin and yang within us; in turn this is affected by the objects with which we surround ourselves, the areas in which we choose to live, and the degree to which we physically alter our natural environment. The scale of problems that could arise varies widely. On an ecological level, the widespread cutting of trees or redirection of watercourses could result in floods or drought. On a personal level, problems could range from rising damp in the home to sleepless nights, or from career problems to minor illnesses. When the feng shui expert is working at an individual level, the worst he may suggest is to move house. However, situations such as this are very rare – usually the changes advised do not require much time or money.

Feng shui has maintained its high profile throughout many parts of the Far East, particularly in Hong Kong, offering solutions to problems in a wide variety of situations. Before the construction of a building begins, a feng shui master, or geomancer, will usually take his place alongside the architect or planner. A full survey may be needed, whether for a fifty-storey office block or a one-bedroom apartment. Or if business is on the decline, a feng shui expert may be called in to take a reading – filing cabinets may need to be moved, or perhaps a doorway should be built in a different part of the wall. Or in the case of a child who seems to be suffering from minor ailments, or is only achieving low grades at school, the answer may lie in the height and size of his or her desk or the positioning of the bed in relation to a window. Even if there is no room to move the bed, or building alterations are not feasible, a partial solution can always be found. A well-placed mirror or a green-leafed plant may bring harmony back into the home.

The History of Feng Shui

The science of feng shui is thought to stem from the close dependence of the Chinese people on the land, crops and climate. Their well-being was inseparable from the productivity of the land and the changing of the seasons. Feng shui was also used to divine suitable burial grounds since it was believed that the fortunes of the living were deeply affected by the well-being of their dead ancestors. If burial grounds were sited in dark hollows or on exposed sites, the spirits of the dead might be unsettled, and in turn living relatives could experience misfortune or suffer from ill health. The link with the dead was further maintained through the annual festival of Ching Ming, when visits were made

to the grave and food offerings given to the dead. This festival is still held today and is regarded as a day of celebration when the family share a meal at the graveside. Consequently, most Chinese burial grounds are sited on south-facing hillsides in order to protect them from the harsh north winds. The hillside itself is usually free from rocky outcrops or ravines to allow the ch'i to circulate smoothly across the land.

The idea of a well-positioned site affecting life's fortunes was also applied to the homes of the living. Ideally it should be south-facing (north-facing in the southern hemisphere), well-protected, with good irrigation, and light or shade as required. Inevitably, not every piece of land could provide ideal conditions, so the feng shui master would suggest ways to enable the ch'i to circulate freely, and also ways to control any malign forces that might arise from stagnant water, steep windy outcrops, waterlogged soil or exposed fields.

Feng shui has been practised for at least three thousand years, although the symbols and philosophies it incorporates date back to an earlier period. Much of the earliest written material on feng shui has not survived, although there are two books still in existence which have influenced feng shui masters to this day: 'The Burial Classics' and 'The Yellow Emperor's Dwelling Classic', dating back from the fourth and fifth centuries AD respectively. The practice of feng shui continued to flourish through the centuries in China. A feng shui expert was known as *hsien-sheng*, a title of respect, and he would often be carried to and from survey sites in a sedan chair. It could be either a full-time or part-time occupation and payment was usually in the form of hospitality rather than a fee.

It could, and still does, take many years to study the art and science of feng shui, a skill that is handed down from master to pupil. Although it can actually be practised by anyone, feng shui experts have a wealth of knowledge at their fingertips; they are a guide to the natural world, and their decisions are thought to have

The shape of the earth dragon is identified in the ridges, slopes and valleys of hills and mountains.

far-reaching effects. Today, a recognized feng shui master can command large sums of money and is far more likely to be found in a suit and tie than wearing the traditional robes.

Although the feng shui master is the only one who can fully relate the shape of the land and buildings to cosmic forces, the practice of feng shui is not his sole prerogative. There are basic surveying skills that anyone can acquire; these skills, combined with common sense and a feel for colour, shape and position, are essential for reading and understanding the environment and your place within it.

The Life and Breath of the Land

Feng shui is rich with signs and symbols, and the art of practising it lies in your ability to read your environment and sense movement and change. Mountain peaks, river valleys and unusual land formations are all identified with an array of animals. The dragon is the most popular, and is not only associated with the land but also with the heavens, the sky, the seas and the emperors of China. According to legend, the dragon is a sign of strength and goodness and is also a symbol of male fertility. It can become visible or invisible at will and can transform itself to appear in different forms wherever it pleases. It can unfurl in the rainclouds or lie coiled in the depths of the sea; it can become as small as a silk-worm, or expand until its presence fills the heavens. And, according to Chinese mythology, there are four dragon kings who rule the seas of the north, south, east and west, the seas that signify the limits of the earth.

The dragon that inhabits the earth is identified in the shape of mountains. Raised features in the land are the veins and arteries of the dragon and ch'i is its blood. Water flowing down a mountain in streams or underground watercourses is likened to ch'i flowing through the ducts of the dragon. There are also hills, pinnacles and peninsulas that resemble tigers, monkeys, dogs and other animals. They could be ready to pounce and devour those nearby, or they could be protectors that bring good fortune to those in their shadow.

The idea of the animal kingdom being reflected in nature's forms brings an added dimension to the natural world. It is full of power where creatures rise up or crouch down, and also where they sleep or where they feed. And it is thought that we are so close to the body of the animal that we cannot fail to be influenced by its form. But it is not only animals that are seen in the shape of the land; rocks can also take on shapes and forms which influence the surrounding area. For example, they may be shaped like pens or books, representing scholarship and conferring academic success on

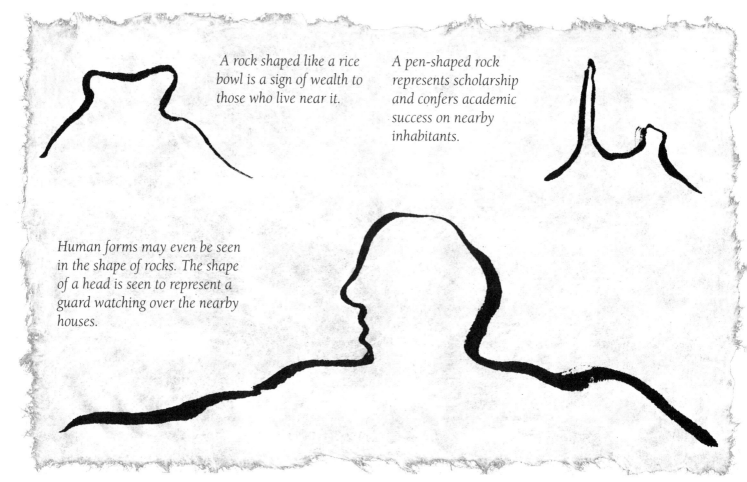

A rock shaped like a rice bowl is a sign of wealth to those who live near it.

A pen-shaped rock represents scholarship and confers academic success on nearby inhabitants.

Human forms may even be seen in the shape of rocks. The shape of a head is seen to represent a guard watching over the nearby houses.

those who live nearby, or perhaps shaped like a rice bowl, a sign of wealth to the inhabitants of the area. Rocks may even take on the form of a human body.

Water is equally as important as the land in maintaining an environmental balance. Rivers are the energetic forces which carry ch'i through the earth; they can also be described as dragons or serpents, and their twists, branches and curves are often referred to as a water dragon. An early feng shui interpretation of river and stream formations can be found in the 'Water Dragon Classic', an ancient text dating back to the sixth century AD. Chapter five includes illustrations that show the lucky and unlucky sites for buildings in relation to the flow of a river, based on these early interpretations.

When the water dragon is not under control it is capable of creating havoc, but when handled carefully it can be a source of fertility. The water dragon can also fly to the heavens to produce rain, influence the tides or affect weather patterns, such as typhoons or drought. In feng shui this mythical creature is very much alive, and needs to be both recognized and respected in order for us to establish a natural balance with the land.

Ch'i

Throughout our lives we are governed by ch'i, the life breath or energy. Our character, movement and health all reflect the circulation of ch'i through our bodies. Ch'i also breathes life into the natural world, enabling rivers to flow, plants to grow and crops to flourish. As well as coursing through land and water, ch'i also gathers and disperses at different spots on the ground; this is known as earth ch'i. The purpose of ch'i was described by the Chinese philosopher Chu Hsi in the twelfth century AD:

Throughout heaven and earth there is Li and there is Ch'i. Li is the Tao (organizing) all forms from above, and the root from which all things are produced. Ch'i is the instrument (composing) all forms from below, and the tools and raw materials with which all things are made. Thus men and all other things must receive this Li at the moment of their coming into being, and thus get their specific nature; so also must they receive this Ch'i and thus get their form.

('Chu Hsi, Collected Works', *Science and Civilisation in China, History of Scientific Thought*, Joseph Needham)

Li determines the order and harmony of life and ch'i breathes life into that order. Just as yin and yang are interdependent, li and ch'i cannot exist without each other. Ch'i is continually increasing and decreasing, prospering and decaying, flowing quickly or becoming stagnant. Your ability to sense the dispersal or accumulation of ch'i in any place is a vital element of your skill in measuring feng shui.

The ch'i that travels through the veins and arteries of the land dragon gives the land its life. Ch'i is quickly dispersed on exposed hill-tops, and through fast-flowing rivers or streams, and accumulates in pools or sluggish water. Lakes and low-lying valleys encourage ch'i to slow down; these are usually places of peace and contemplation and as such are a reflection of yin. Fields or outcrops exposed to the wind have a more forceful and active aura and are a reflection of yang.

When ch'i moves through a room or house it creates a pleasant and welcoming atmosphere: there will be a balanced amount of light and the temperature will be pleasant, and any colours will appear neither too bright nor too dull. Without realizing it you may be able to sense the positive movement of ch'i in a specific place – it gives you a sense of well-being and harmony.

While ch'i breathes life into a certain area it can also disperse and decay allowing *sha* to enter. Sha is the breath that takes life away – the opposite of ch'i – and is a negative force. It can accumulate in stagnant water or in poorly drained soil. It rises from the earth, or is manifest in sharp, cold winds that penetrate protecting walls or outcrops. There is another type of sha that travels along both natural and man-made straight lines, such as rivers, canals, and railway and telephone lines. Its influence can be held back by a fence, screen or row of trees. The results of the accumulation of sha affect not only the landscape but also individual health and wealth.

Heaven Ch'i

There is another aspect of ch'i which governs the cycle of the seasons and it is known as *heaven ch'i*. The year is divided into four seasons – spring, summer, autumn and winter – but it is also divided into six phases – heaven ch'i – which mark the expansion and contraction of ch'i throughout the year. These six phases are broken down again into twenty-four terms which denote various climatic, agricultural and solar patterns (*see right*).

This process of movement, gathering and decline is also represented in the dynamic interaction of yin and yang. As spring approaches, yang begins to grow and yin to decline. Yang reaches its peak at the height of summer and then goes into decline, to be replaced by yin, which begins its ascendency as autumn draws in and reaches its full strength in the winter months.

The I Ching

The process of change and interaction between yin and yang is illustrated in an ancient Chinese divination text called the *I Ching*, or *Book of Changes*. The trigrams, figures of three broken or unbroken lines, which are contained in the *I Ching* have been attributed to Fu Hsi, a mythological character who brought the gift of civilization to the world. It is said that the Yellow Dragon which emerged from the River Lo gave the elements of writing to Emperor Fu Hsi. Beyond the legends that surround the *I Ching* no one can be sure about its age or author, although its system of divination dates back before 1100 BC.

The Phases of Heaven Ch'i	The 24 Terms of the Solar Calendar (二十四节气)
Growing ch'i	Beginning of spring 立春 Rain water 雨水 Excited insects 惊蛰 Spring equinox 春分
Expanding ch'i	Clear and bright 清明 Grain rains 谷雨 Summer begins 立夏 Grain filling 小满
Full-grown ch'i	Grain in ear 芒种 Summer solstice 夏至 Slight heat 小暑 Great heat 大暑
Changing ch'i	Autumn begins 立秋 Limit of heat 处暑 White dew 白露 Autumn equinox 秋分
Gathered ch'i	Cold dew 寒露 Hoar frost descends 霜降 Winter begins 立冬 Slight snow 小雪
Hidden ch'i	Great snow 大雪 Winter solstice 冬至 Slight cold 小寒 Great cold 大寒

Yin and yang are traditionally represented by straight lines. It is thought that the origin of these lines lies in the cracks that appeared on ancient tortoise-shell oracles. When help was needed to make decisions or guidance required for the future, a hole was drilled into a tortoise shell and a heated stick placed into the dent. The cracks that appeared in the shell were read by a shaman, an intermediary between the human world and the spirit world.

In the *I Ching*, yin is represented by a broken line (▬▬) and yang by an unbroken line (▬▬). When three yin or yang lines are placed on top of one another they form what is known as a trigram. There are a total of eight trigrams, and each one represents an element of nature (*see right*).

If the trigrams are placed into sets of two to form six lines there are sixty-four possible combinations, and these are called hexagrams (*see page 26*). Each hexagram in the *I Ching* is accompanied by a cryptic judgement, such as Origin, Obstruction, Inner Confidence or Not Yet Done. These brief judgements have been attributed to King Wen who ruled a small Chinese state in 1160 BC. Further commentaries were reputedly added by his son, the Duke of Chou, and just over five hundred years later Confucius added other observations to the hexagrams. Thus the traditional interpretations of these hexagrams have developed gradually over the centuries.

The position of the yin and yang lines in each hexagram represents their continual interaction and dynamism. They reflect the fact that we are constantly in a state of change, and it is through this process that we also follow the natural and eternal order known as the Way, or the Tao. The Tao speaks of flowing with nature, bending in the face of obstacles and of having the wisdom to recognize nature's path, not just in the world around us but also within ourselves. Feng shui is a way of learning to travel with the flow of the Tao, and *The Feng Shui Kit* will enable you to learn the basics of understanding feng shui in *your* environment. The next chapter will soon show you how.

Trigram	Name	Element
	Li	fire
	K'un	earth
	Tui	marsh
	Ch'ien	heaven
	K'an	water
	Ken	mountain
	Chen	thunder
	Sun	wind

CHAPTER TWO

BEFORE YOU BEGIN

Long Life

Anyone who is experienced in feng shui is able to sense where ch'i is circulating by the shape and fertility of the land or the shape and layout of the building that is being surveyed. The traditional feng shui compass shown here is used to give a more detailed reading and can have more than thirty concentric rings. The symbols inscribed on each ring represent both real and imaginary forces, phenomena and creatures. Such a detailed compass could be regarded as a physical representation of the cosmos.

The simplified and specially designed eight-ringed compass provided in *The Feng Shui Kit* has retained many traditional Chinese signs and symbols to help you identify fortunate directions and assess the balance of yin and yang in a particular area. It is used in the same way as a traditional compass to assess whether a room, house or piece of furniture is in a positive position. You can also stand outside a building or an architectural feature to take a reading for the whole structure. You will be able to use the information contained in the later chapters to help you understand the significance of the shapes of natural features, roads, rivers and buildings so that you can build up a detailed reading of your surroundings.

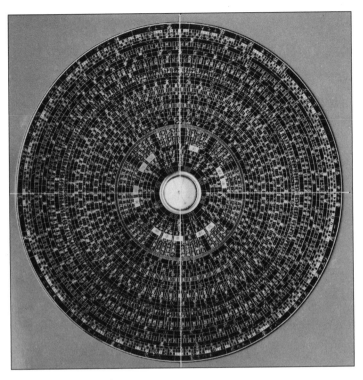

A traditional feng shui compass.

As you work through each ring of the compass there are suggestions to help you remedy negative readings. If you find that negative readings recur you should try a new direction. The compass is your guide but since choice of colour, shape and design also depends on individual taste you should always use the compass in conjunction with your own judgement and intuition. But first, there are some personal details to be worked out before you use *The Feng Shui Kit* compass, so that its use is more meaningful.

Finding Your Personal Lucky and Unlucky Directions

Your lucky and unlucky directions make up what is called your personal *Pa Tzu* compass, and you need to know which of eight possibles shown overleaf on pages 18–19 is yours, so that you can quickly refer to it as you use *The Feng Shui Kit* compass. This is how you calculate your personal Pa Tzu compass. There are two different formulae, one for males and one for females.

Calculations for Males

● Subtract the last two numbers of your year of birth from 100 and divide by 9.
● The remainder is the number of your compass.
● If there is no remainder you should take compass number 9.

Example: Born in 1962 ● 100 − 62 = 38
● 38 ÷ 9 = 4 remainder 2
● Your Pa Tzu compass is number 2

Calculations for Females

● Subtract 4 from the last two numbers of your year of birth and divide by 9.
● The remainder is the number of your compass.
● If there is no remainder you should take compass number 9.

Example: Born in 1962 ● 62 − 4 = 58
● 58 ÷ 9 = 6 remainder 4
● Your Pa Tzu compass is number 4.

The Pa Tzu Compasses: EASTERN LIFE

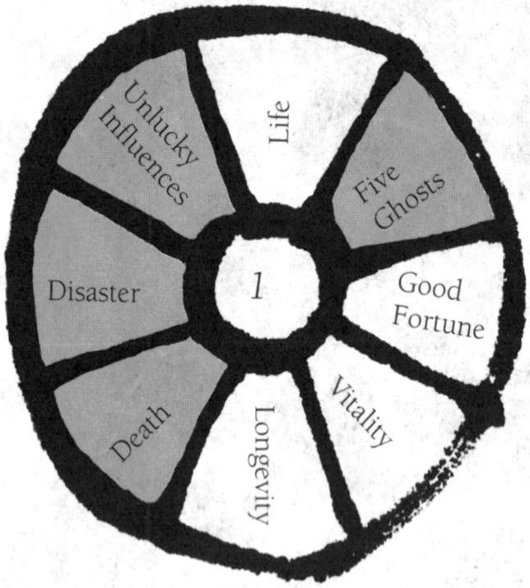

Pa Tzu Compass No 1

Element: water

Trigram: K'an

☐ Lucky Directions

▨ Unlucky Directions

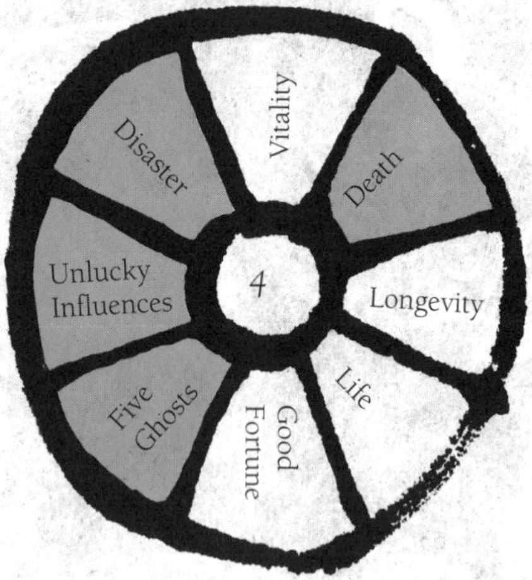

Pa Tzu Compass No 4

Element: wood

Trigram: Sun

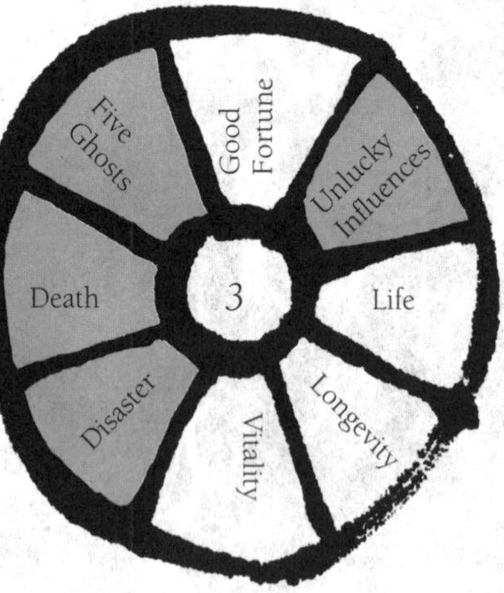

Pa Tzu Compass No 3

Element: wood

Trigram: Chen

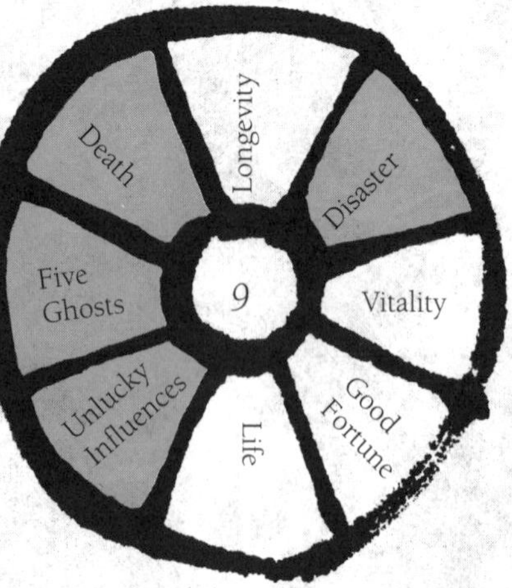

Pa Tzu Compass No 9

Element: fire

Trigram: Li

The Pa Tzu Compasses: WESTERN LIFE

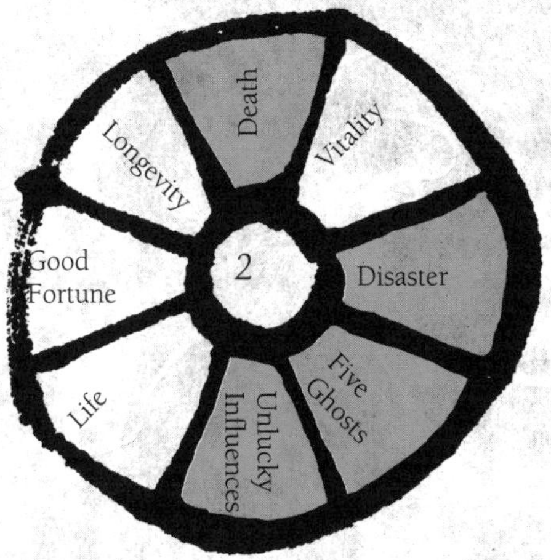

Pa Tzu Compass No 2

Element: earth

Trigram: K'un

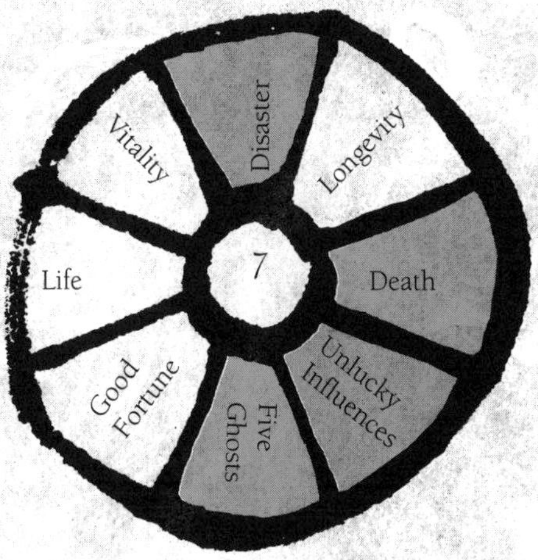

Pa Tzu Compass No 7

Element: metal

Trigram: Tui

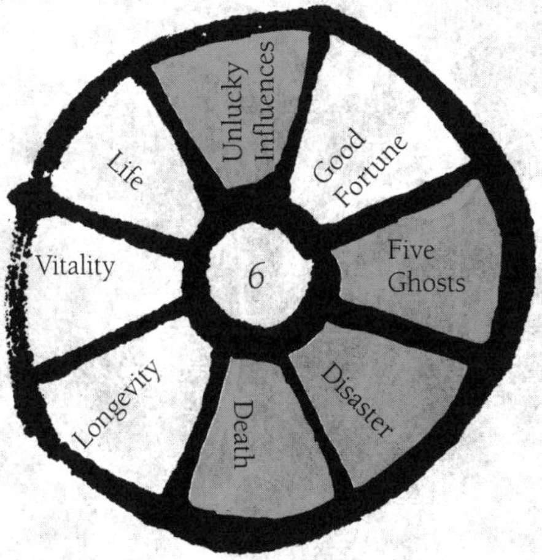

☐ *Lucky Directions*

▨ *Unlucky Directions*

Pa Tzu Compass No 6

Element: metal

Trigram: Ch'ien

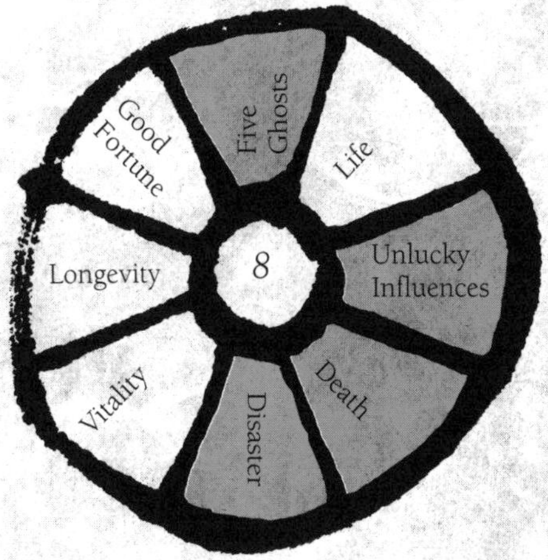

Pa Tzu Compass No 8

Element: earth

Trigram: Ken

By referring to the diagrams you will have found which compass matches your personal number. You now need to make a note of the following information.

If your Pa Tzu compass number is one, three, four or nine you belong to the *Eastern Life* group. Your lucky directions are east, south-east, north and south. If your Pa Tzu compass number is two, six, seven, or eight you belong to the *Western Life* group. Your lucky directions are west, south-west, north-west and north-east.

The number five is traditionally associated with the centre of a compass. In Chinese geomancy, the centre is considered an essential direction but it does not have its own particular forecast, as do the other eight Pa Tzu compasses. If your calculations produce the number five you should use one of the following compasses: number two for males, and number eight for females.

When you look at *The Feng Shui Kit* compass you will notice that some of the directions listed in the second ring are shaded gold in order to separate those which belong to the Eastern Life group from those of the Western Life group, and to help you recognize your lucky directions.

Finding Your Personal Element and Trigram

Each of the eight Pa Tzu compasses has its own personal element and trigram. These are listed along with their corresponding compass on the previous pages.

Wood, fire, earth, metal and water are the five elements of Chinese astrology. It is thought that they are alive in every substance and are part of the process of change. It is the interaction between the elements that helps a feng shui expert decide whether a certain place is likely to be lucky or unlucky.

The trigrams are made up of three lines which are either broken or unbroken: the broken lines are yin and the unbroken lines are yang. Yin and yang are dynamic forces that shape and balance all life in the universe. They are both present in our emotions, health and actions; in plants, animals, nature and the heavens. In fact, they are present in different amounts in everything that we see and cannot see. Nothing remains absolutely yin or absolutely yang; they are changing as our world is changing. This is why the yin and yang lines are in different positions in each of the trigrams.

Finding Your Personal Chinese Animal Sign

Your Chinese animal sign corresponds to your year of birth, and you can discover which of twelve animals you are from the chart on the opposite page. It is important that you take note of the date on which the Chinese new year begins, as your date of birth may belong to the animal sign of the previous year. The chart covers the years 1900–2019.

Chart of Chinese Animal Signs

Year of Birth	Chinese Year Begins	Chinese Animal	Year of Birth	Chinese Year Begins	Chinese Animal	Year of Birth	Chinese Year Begins	Chinese Animal	Year of Birth	Chinese Year Begins	Chinese Animal
1900	Jan 31st	Rat	1930	Jan 30th	Horse	1960	Jan 28th	Rat	1990	Jan 27th	Horse
1901	Feb 19th	Ox	1931	Feb 17th	Ram	1961	Feb 15th	Ox	1991	Feb 15th	Ram
1902	Feb 8th	Tiger	1932	Feb 6th	Monkey	1962	Feb 5th	Tiger	1992	Feb 4th	Monkey
1903	Jan 29th	Rabbit	1933	Jan 26th	Rooster	1963	Jan 25th	Rabbit	1993	Jan 23rd	Rooster
1904	Feb 16th	Dragon	1934	Feb 14th	Dog	1964	Feb 13th	Dragon	1994	Feb 10th	Dog
1905	Feb 4th	Snake	1935	Feb 4th	Pig	1965	Feb 2nd	Snake	1995	Jan 31st	Pig
1906	Jan 25th	Horse				1966	Jan 21st	Horse			
1907	Feb 13th	Ram	1936	Jan 24th	Rat	1967	Feb 9th	Ram	1996	Feb 19th	Rat
1908	Feb 2nd	Monkey	1937	Feb 11th	Ox	1968	Jan 30th	Monkey	1997	Feb 7th	Ox
1909	Jan 22nd	Rooster	1938	Jan 31st	Tiger	1969	Feb 17th	Rooster	1998	Jan 28th	Tiger
1910	Feb 10th	Dog	1939	Feb 19th	Rabbit	1970	Feb 6th	Dog	1999	Feb 16th	Rabbit
1911	Jan 30th	Pig	1940	Feb 8th	Dragon	1971	Jan 27th	Pig	2000	Feb 5th	Dragon
			1941	Jan 27th	Snake				2001	Jan 24th	Snake
1912	Feb 18th	Rat	1942	Feb 18th	Horse	1972	Feb 15th	Rat	2002	Feb 12th	Horse
1913	Feb 6th	Ox	1943	Feb 5th	Ram	1973	Feb 3rd	Ox	2003	Feb 1st	Ram
1914	Jan 26th	Tiger	1944	Jan 25th	Monkey	1974	Jan 23rd	Tiger	2004	Jan 22nd	Monkey
1915	Feb 14th	Rabbit	1945	Feb 13th	Rooster	1975	Feb 11th	Rabbit	2005	Feb 9th	Rooster
1916	Feb 3rd	Dragon	1946	Feb 2nd	Dog	1976	Jan 31st	Dragon	2006	Jan 29th	Dog
1917	Jan 23rd	Snake	1947	Jan 22nd	Pig	1977	Feb 18th	Snake	2007	Feb 18th	Pig
1918	Feb 11th	Horse				1978	Feb 7th	Horse			
1919	Feb 1st	Ram	1948	Feb 10th	Rat	1979	Jan 28th	Ram	2008	Feb 7th	Rat
1920	Feb 20th	Monkey	1949	Jan 29th	Ox	1980	Feb 16th	Monkey	2009	Jan 26th	Ox
1921	Feb 8th	Rooster	1950	Feb 17th	Tiger	1981	Feb 5th	Rooster	2010	Feb 14th	Tiger
1922	Jan 28th	Dog	1951	Feb 6th	Rabbit	1982	Jan 25th	Dog	2011	Feb 3rd	Rabbit
1923	Feb 16th	Pig	1952	Jan 27th	Dragon	1983	Feb 13th	Pig	2012	Jan 23rd	Dragon
			1953	Feb 14th	Snake				2013	Feb 10th	Snake
1924	Feb 5th	Rat	1954	Feb 3rd	Horse	1984	Feb 2nd	Rat	2014	Jan 31st	Horse
1925	Jan 24th	Ox	1955	Jan 24th	Ram	1985	Feb 20th	Ox	2015	Feb 19th	Ram
1926	Feb 13th	Tiger	1956	Feb 12th	Monkey	1986	Feb 9th	Tiger	2016	Feb 8th	Monkey
1927	Feb 2nd	Rabbit	1957	Jan 31st	Rooster	1987	Jan 29th	Rabbit	2017	Jan 28th	Rooster
1928	Jan 23rd	Dragon	1958	Feb 18th	Dog	1988	Feb 17th	Dragon	2018	Feb 16th	Dog
1929	Feb 10th	Snake	1959	Feb 8th	Pig	1989	Feb 6th	Snake	2019	Feb 5th	Pig

CHAPTER THREE

Using the Compass

Prosperity

You can use *The Feng Shui Kit* compass to take a reading for any direction or feature inside or outside a building. The compass can be used on its own, although you will be able to gain a more detailed personal reading when it is combined with the readings from your personal Pa Tzu compass. For ease of understanding, it will be assumed that your first reading is taken indoors.

The main compass has two dials. The inner dial, which has six rings, has to be moved first to give you information about a particular direction. Once you have lined up the inner dial following the steps below you then turn the outer dial, which has two rings, so that the Chinese animal sign corresponding to your year of birth is lined up with your reading. You will then be able to take individual readings from each ring of the dial.

The centre of the main compass, which contains the compass needle, is known in feng shui as Heaven's Pool. Heaven's Pool symbolizes the starting point for ch'i. It is in this area that yin and yang interact with each other, waxing and waning, rising and falling. Since yin and yang give rise to the change and pattern of life, the centre of the compass also represents the centre of the universe. In traditional Chinese feng shui the tip of the compass needle points to the south. On the compass provided the tip of the needle points north, in accordance with usage in the West.

There are divisions marked on the edges of the compass which represent ruler measurements; these are used later in your feng shui reading (*see page 71*).

Making a Reading

Hold the compass flat in the palms of your hands or place it on an even surface. It should be facing the direction you want to assess. It does not matter which way round you hold the compass, but make sure that a straight edge and not a corner is facing the direction of your reading so that one of the nylon threads is pointing towards the direction you are assessing. You should also make sure that you are not too close to metal objects or metal tables since this will confuse the compass needle. Hold the compass still to allow the needle to settle on a north/south axis.

Step One: The Inner Dial
There are two moving dials on the compass. At this stage you should only turn the inner dial. There is a red line painted across the centre of Heaven's Pool, below the needle; this needs to line up with the needle from north to south. As you turn the dial this line will move at the same time. Keep turning the dial slowly until the red line lies directly under the compass needle and is on the same north/south axis as the needle (the end with the two red dots should be aligned underneath the tail – the white end – of the compass needle). You are now ready to take a reading from the compass.

The reading for this direction, comprising trigram,

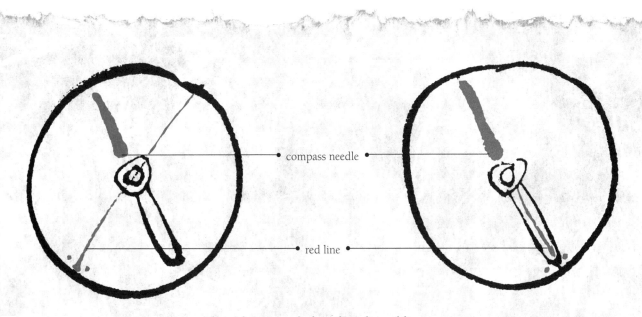

compass needle

red line

Turn the inner dial so that the red line is
aligned under the compass needle with the two red dots
underneath the tail (white end) of the needle.

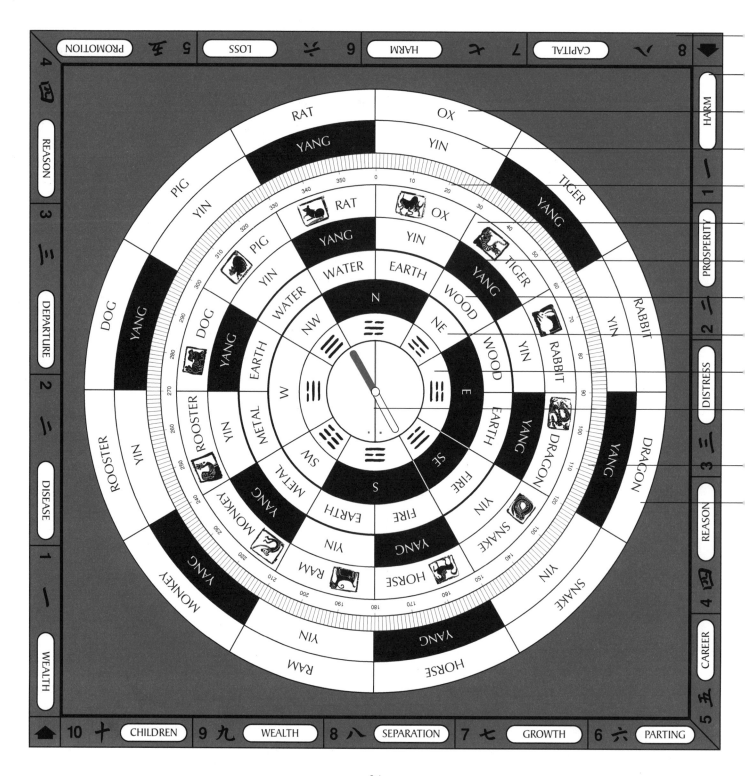

— *ruler markings: outdoor categories (numbers 1–8)*

— *ruler markings: indoor categories (numbers 1–10)*

• *ring eight: the twelve animals*

• *ring seven: yin and yang*

• *ring six: the compass degrees*

• *ring five : the twelve animals*

• *ring four: yin and yang*

• *ring three: the elements*

• *ring two: the directions*

• *ring one: the trigrams*

• *red line on base of centre compass*
  (align two red dots under tail of needle to take reading)

• *inner dial*

• *outer dial*

The Feng Shui Kit *compass. This simplified eight-ringed compass has two dials. The inner dial turns along with the magnetic compass in the centre and gives you information relating to a particular direction. The outer dial moves freely so you can align your own Chinese animal sign with the details for the direction you are assessing. The ruler markings along the edges allow you to measure anything in your environment and obtain an instant positive or negative reading (see page 71).*

lucky or unlucky direction, element, yin or yang, Chinese animal and the compass degrees, lies under the piece of nylon thread that is furthest away from you and pointing in the direction that you are facing.

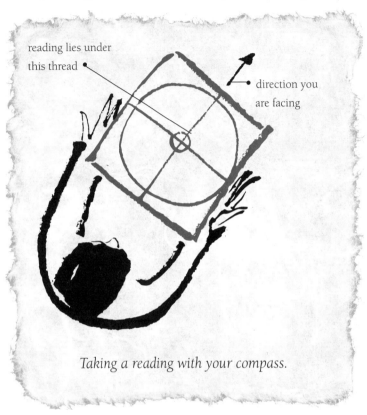

reading lies under this thread

direction you are facing

Taking a reading with your compass.

Step Two: The Outer Dial

Holding the inner dial in place, so that you do not lose the reading you have just made, move the outer dial so that your personal Chinese animal sign is lined up underneath the nylon thread to match your compass reading. Now you are ready to interpret your reading.

Ring One: The Trigrams

Make a note of the trigram that appears on the compass dial under the nylon thread; you should have already made a note of the trigram that belongs to your personal Pa Tzu compass. These two trigrams combine to form a hexagram, and there are two possible hexagrams that can be applied to your reading depending on which trigram constitutes the lower trigram and which constitutes the upper trigram.

There are two different sequences in which the trigrams can be arranged. When they were first arranged in an octagonal shape they followed an order known as the Former Heaven Sequence. This sequence is traditionally attributed to Fu Hsi who, according to Chinese mythology, brought the gifts of civilization to the world. The arrangement of trigrams on traditional feng shui compasses and *pa kua* mirrors (*see page 70*) usually follows this sequence, although the trigrams on *The Feng Shui Kit* compass have been arranged according to an order known as the Later Heaven Sequence. This sequence is believed to date back more than three thousand years and is attributed to King Wen, the author of the cryptic descriptions that accompany each hexagram. The order of trigrams reflects the balance of yin and yang at particular areas on the ground. The Later Heaven Sequence is also the order which is used in the Pa Tzu system, so it has been used on *The Feng Shui Kit* compass to ensure maximum clarity when you are taking a reading.

The sixty-four hexagrams formed by the pairing of the trigrams are contained in the *I Ching*, or *Book of Changes*, an ancient Chinese divination text. Each hexagram is associated with a short reading which you can use and interpret in your own way. The readings are not meant to give you a definitive answer; instead they illustrate the fact that everything is constantly changing according to a natural order. They are a guide to the fortune, or otherwise, of the direction you are assessing, and as such should be read and understood in relation to your character and circumstances. You should refer to the readings for both hexagrams and follow the advice of that which is most appropriate to your situation.

Read along the chart shown opposite to find the numbers of your hexagrams. Individual readings for the sixty-four hexagrams appear on the following pages 28–43. Ring two follows on page 44.

Upper Trigram		Ch'ien	Chen	K'an	Ken	K'un	Sun	Li	Tui
Lower Trigram									
	Ch'ien	1	34	5	26	11	9	14	43
	Chen	25	51	3	27	24	42	21	17
	K'an	6	40	29	4	7	59	64	47
	Ken	33	62	39	52	15	53	56	31
	K'un	12	16	8	23	2	20	35	45
	Sun	44	32	48	18	46	57	50	28
	Li	13	55	63	22	36	37	30	49
	Tui	10	54	60	41	19	61	38	58

The Hexagrams of the I Ching

1. Ch'ien

This hexagram is called Origin, and the trigram Ch'ien, heaven, appears twice.

It indicates the beginning of everything and implies harmony and peace. Since it is made up of six yang lines it also represents strength and power. It is said that the Ch'ien hexagram enables everything to find its appropriate place and to flourish.

2. K'un

This hexagram is called Success, and the trigram K'un, earth, appears twice.

It represents soft and gentle characteristics, and its calm and peaceful nature is symbolized by a female horse. The six yin lines in this hexagram give it a tender quality and at the same time imply healthy growth and vitality.

3. Chun

This hexagram is called Birth Pangs, and combines the trigrams K'an and Chen, water and thunder.

It warns of the need for careful thought before starting a new venture. It indicates a potentially dangerous and confused time which is why it is advisable to tread carefully and seek good advice. There is, however, the opportunity for success and persistence will win through in the end.

4. Meng

This hexagram is called Rebellious Youth, and combines the trigrams Ken and K'an, mountain and water.

At the moment the situation looks chaotic and it may be hard to make a decision. This hexagram could be compared to a young child who is confused by the adult world, but in time the situation will calm down and everything will become much clearer. A certain amount of patience and inner strength may be needed now, so do not rush ahead in the excitement of the moment.

5. Hsü

This hexagram is called Patience, and combines the trigrams K'an and Ch'ien, water and heaven.

 It is said that the shape of this hexagram is like a cloud rising from the earth, and is indicative of the interdependence of the cloud and the earth. In the same way our physical and emotional needs are dependent on each other; it is important that there is a balance between work and play. This hexagram also refers to difficulties ahead, so study your surroundings carefully and you will be able to solve any problems with care and patience.

6. Sung

This hexagram is called Contention, and combines the trigrams Ch'ien and K'an, heaven and water.

The lines in this hexagram imply the struggle that is neccesary to achieve success. In the lower half of the hexagram there is an air of danger but in the top half there is wisdom and good judgement. Do not give in easily; pursue your aims but beware as your plans could fail if you approach projects carelessly.

7. Shih

This hexagram is called The Army, and combines the trigrams K'un and K'an, earth and water.

The lines symbolize powerful people willing to take responsibility, not just for individuals but for the general good. The emphasis here is on a good leader who can fire others with respect and enthusiasm. This hexagram indicates that great things can be achieved with co-operation and sound guidance.

8. Pi

This hexagram is called Unity, and combines the trigrams K'an and K'un, water and earth.

There is a feeling of danger in the lower part of this hexagram although the top half is relaxed and calm. It indicates a crowd of people who will be successful if they work in co-operation. Any problems that arise must be ironed out quickly and fairly, or else they could prove destructive. You should ask others for their opinion even if you feel you are absolutely right.

小畜

9. Hsiao Ch'u

This hexagram is called Holding Back the Less Able, and combines the trigrams Sun and Ch'ien, wind and heaven.

 This hexagram is thought to indicate clouds moving across the sky; although there is no sign of rain at the moment, a heavy downpour may be on its way. Thought should be given to the future and adequate preparations made. The storm to come cannot maintain its force for long; you need to be inwardly determined and strong, and outwardly open and approachable. Others should realize that you are open to compromise, but do not lose sight of your original vision.

履

10. Li

This hexagram is called Walking Carefully, and combines the trigrams Ch'ien and Tui, heaven and marsh.

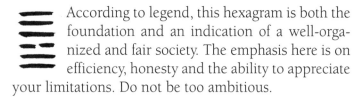 According to legend, this hexagram is both the foundation and an indication of a well-organized and fair society. The emphasis here is on efficiency, honesty and the ability to appreciate your limitations. Do not be too ambitious.

泰

11. T'ai

This hexagram is called Benevolence, and combines the trigrams K'un and Ch'ien, earth and heaven.

 This is a positive combination which produces peace and harmony and it is likened to a successful relationship between a man and a woman. There is a good balance between strength and thoughtfulness, and determination and patience. This combination should give you confidence and contentment.

否

12. P'i

This hexagram is called Obstruction, and combines the trigrams Ch'ien and K'un, heaven and earth.

There is a sense of these two trigrams pulling away from each other. Energy appears to be at a low ebb and it is hard to know which direction to take. It is said that this hexagram is like scattered sand which cannot bind together, and accordingly the prospects ahead are bleak. You may find it hard to make a final decision, or circumstances may prevent you from doing so. A strong will and patience are needed now.

13. T'ung Jen

This hexagram is called Companions, and combines the trigrams Ch'ien and Li, heaven and fire.

This a positive combination as it refers to a group of people working in harmony. Although there is a good sense of unity, inevitably there will be differences of opinion so it is important that one person leads the others. Whoever makes the final decision must be trusted by the others and act on their wishes.

大有
14. Ta Yu

This hexagram is called Many Possessions, and combines the trigrams Li and Chi'en, fire and heaven.

When these trigrams are combined they are a source of strength and encouragement. There is an element of obstinacy and awkwardness in the upper trigram, but this is helped by the powerful and productive qualities of the lower trigram. Although determination and strength are important qualities they can be softened and improved by listening to others. With care problems will be resolved, so do not rush ahead with change.

15. Ch'ien

This hexagram is called Modesty, and combines the trigrams K'un and Ken, earth and mountain.

This hexagram indicates the importance of consideration for others, particularly if you are in a position of authority. Bear in mind that the plans you make will affect others, and when others praise your work you should accept their praise with humility.

16. Yü

This hexagram is called Enthusiasm, and combines the trigrams Chen and K'un, thunder and earth.

A successful period is on the way. This hexagram is likened to the relationship between a mother and an older son; the son does not always follow his mother's advice but with compromise on either side the problems will be resolved. Co-operation and shared enthusiasm are essential in order for a project to progress.

17. Sui

This hexagram is called Reaching an Agreement, and combines the trigrams Tui and Chen, marsh and thunder.

The Tui trigram has a peaceful nature while Chen is powerful and active. This hexagram is likened to thunder rolling across a marsh causing the water to ripple. In time rain will fall on the marsh, which in turn will irrigate the surrounding land; in effect, the appearance of the thunder sets a chain of events into action. This hexagram indicates that the time is right to follow the guidance of another; it is a time of change when the old is replaced by the new.

18. Ku

This hexagram is called Decay, and combines Ken and Sun, mountain and wind.

It is wise to remember that we pass through cycles of good and bad times; it is said that heaven's way is made up of endings and beginnings. This hexagram has a rebellious nature and signifies a time of disorder, but there is also the possibility of hope. It is best to start afresh and someone with good judgement will offer support.

19. Lin

This hexagram is called To Draw Near, and combines the trigrams K'un and Tui, earth and marsh.

This hexagram signifies a productive and encouraging time. It symbolizes earth becoming fertile with water from the marsh. This is the time for someone with experience and education to pass on encouragement and advice, and for those with less experience to listen.

20. Kuan

This hexagram is called Examine, and combines the trigrams Sun and K'un, wind and earth.

This hexagram is sometimes likened to an important official who has prepared well and is keeping watch on those who work for him. Think carefully before you act; it is important that you are in the right frame of mind before you make a decision. If you are going to make any changes take into account the natural environment and work with it not against it.

噬嗑

21. Shih Ho

This hexagram is called Biting Through, and combines the trigrams Li and Chen, fire and thunder.

The combination of Li and Chen produces thunder and lightning. There is a warning in this hexagram against the dangers of excess, whether in food, furniture or entertainment. The desire to have everything as and when you want it is likely to lead to misfortune; you need to exercise restraint in order to achieve success.

贲

22. Pi

This hexagram is called To Adorn, and combines the trigrams Ken and Li, mountain and fire.

Everyday life is enhanced by an appreciation of culture; we need it to brighten our lives. But beware of becoming too extravagant or ostentatious, and in the process failing to see the beauty in simpler designs or colours.

剥

23. Po

This hexagram is called Peeling or Splitting, and combines the trigrams Ken and K'un, mountain and earth.

The earth at the lower part of this hexagram is not firm enough to support the mountain that sits above it and eventually it will collapse. This hexagram heralds a time of uncertainty and disintegration. Take time to plan for the future, but do not carry out any important changes at this time.

复

24. Fu

This hexagram is called Return, and combines the trigrams K'un and Chen, earth and thunder.

This hexagram indicates a period of growth after a period of disorder and disintegration. It is a positive hexagram and is full of possibilities. It is time for a fresh start so enlist the help of others, but do not try to rush change as it will take a natural course.

无妄

25. Wu Wang

This hexagram is called Honesty, and combines the trigrams Ch'ien and Chen, heaven and thunder.

It is said that the path of Wu Wang is natural and just, and anyone who follows this hexagram follows a natural course set out for them. This hexagram warns against attempting the impossible. Do not distress yourself thinking about events that you cannot control or objects you cannot possess; be content with what you have.

大畜

26. Ta Ch'u

This hexagram is called Great Powers of Domestication, and combines the trigrams Ken and Ch'ien, mountain and heaven.

Heaven in the midst of a mountain is an indication of accumulated treasures which can and should be used for the benefit of others. It is the time to make use of things which have not yet been used or have been stored for the future. Others should be able to share what you have acquired.

27. I

This hexagram is called Taking Nourishment, and combines the trigrams Ken and Chen, mountain and thunder.

It is said that the top and bottom lines of this hexagram are shaped like lips and the inner four lines are like teeth. While food is important for survival we also need to be nourished by good intention or action. There is a warning in this hexagram against over-indulgence and extravagance; do not push yourself or others too far – try to find a natural balance.

大过

28. Ta Kuo

This hexagram is called Great Experience, and combines the trigrams Tui and Sun, marsh and wind.

The four inner yang lines of this hexagram are strong and likened to a beam, but the two outer lines are weak and have difficulty supporting the weight of the beam. There are changes ahead but they may come at a time when your resources are already over-stretched. Do not waste your energies on inappropriate projects; concentrate instead on work that is likely to bear fruit.

29. K'an

This hexagram is called The Watery Depths, and the trigram K'an, water, appears twice.

 It is said that the two yang lines are like rivers in a deep ravine which continue to flow regardless of the obstacles that stand in their way. Do not be too ambitious if you are attempting something new as you may be overwhelmed by events. Work with the objects and people you know and trust, and confront the difficulties ahead with patience.

31. Hsien

This hexagram is called All-embracing, and combines the trigrams Tui and Ken, marsh and mountain.

Since the marsh rests on the mountain its moisture is able to nourish the land below. Determination and flexibility are combined in this hexagram to produce a strong partnership. If you give advice you must be equally prepared to listen. Do not rush headlong into new plans or changes; patience and reflection are advised.

30. Li

This hexagram is called To Shine Brightly or To Part, and the trigram Li, fire, appears twice.

This hexagram represents light and civilization. The sun, which is represented in the trigram Li, illuminates the earth during the day and reflects onto the moon at night. This hexagram emphasizes the importance of natural order and, similarly, it will be productive for you to work in harmony with the natural features that surround you. Consideration and careful planning are essential.

32. Heng

This hexagram is called Constant, and combines the trigrams Chen and Sun, thunder and wind.

This hexagram has a strong and durable nature and is sometimes compared to the sun and moon, which ceaselessly illuminate the earth. Reflect on your needs and your relationship with the environment around you, and you will be unlikely to make a mistake. Approach any changes gradually, and do not expect immediate success.

遯

33. Tun

This hexagram is called To Hide, and combines the trigrams Ch'ien and Ken, heaven and mountain.

The two yin lines at the bottom of the hexagram are likely to cause trouble for the yang lines above. This is a time for thought and not for action. If you are planning to change anything consider the implications for others first and then proceed slowly.

大壯

34. Ta Chuang

This hexagram is called Great Strength, and combines the trigrams Chen and Ch'ien, thunder and heaven.

The energy and power of thunder work well with the natural order of heaven. This is a positive time when doubts and worries will fade into the background. Make the most of this opportunity to carry out plans that you have been considering, but beware of being too confident as you may offend others.

晋

35. Chin

This hexagram is called To Advance, and combines the trigrams Li and K'un, fire and earth.

There are times when you find it hard to realize your ideas; it could be because you are demanding too much or others are blocking your plans. It is important not to despair because you will eventually succeed. There is a note of prosperity in this hexagram but this good fortune should be shared, so try to create an environment which will be welcoming to others.

明夷

36. Ming I

This hexagram is called Brightness Dimmed, and combines the trigrams K'un and Li, earth and fire.

In this hexagram the light of the fire is shadowed by the darkness of the earth, although this does not detract from the beauty of the fire. This could be a confusing time and you are likely to find it difficult to organize yourself or make a final decision. Take time to decide what suits you instead of allowing yourself to be swept along by events. If you are put under pressure, rely on your own intuition and taste.

37. Chia Jen

This hexagram is called The Family, and combines the trigrams Sun and Li, wind and fire.

 There is an emphasis here on the influence of feminine form or style. A balance is needed between the organization of your home and the wider environment. Do not plan in isolation, and make sure you take into account the needs of those living with you as well as the natural features that surround you.

39. Chien

This hexagram is called Difficulty, and combines the trigrams K'an and Ken, water and mountain.

Assess your surroundings very carefully before you spend money or use energy. You need to be aware of possible pitfalls, but do not deliberate too long in case you lose a sense of creativity or excitement. Consult others before you make a choice as their suggestions could be invaluable.

38. K'uei

This hexagram is called Opposition, and combines the trigrams Li and Tui, fire and marsh.

The fire and the marsh appear to be in opposition to each other; while the flames travel upwards the water from the marsh seeps down. They can, however, work together since fire warms earth and water nourishes earth. This hexagram is likened to a friendship or partnership that is able to carry out small ventures but does not work well on a larger scale. It may be a time of uncertainty, so do not lose control of your original vision or plan.

40. Hsieh

This hexagram is called Release, and combines the trigrams Chen and K'an, thunder and water.

There is an air of foreboding in this hexagram, but there is also the possibility of release from a difficult situation. The lines are likened to a sky that is becoming clear after a thunderstorm. It could be that you feel trapped or compromised but this is likely to pass. If you are given the freedom to follow your own instincts, try to stop and consider the suggestions that others make.

41. Sun

This hexagram is called Injured, and combines the trigrams Ken and Tui, mountain and marsh.

 It appears that many demands are being made on both your time and your money. But eventually, in ways that you least expect, your efforts will be repaid. This hexagram indicates that changes in fortune are on the way; to be secure it may be better to curb your spending and be satisfied with what you have, so your money is safe for when you need to finance a special project.

益

42. I

This hexagram is called Increase, and combines the trigrams Sun and Chen, wind and thunder.

This hexagram indicates a time of change and co-operation. There is a strong sense of movement and progress here; it could be movement from one place to another, or the overcoming of barriers that stand in your way. You do not need to impress your ideas or designs on anyone as the way ahead is clear and full of possibilities.

夬

43. Kuai

This hexagram is called New Outcome, and combines the trigrams Tui and Ch'ien, marsh and heaven.

 This hexagram indicates a move towards establishing harmony in a certain place or with others. Honesty with yourself and those around you is your best policy at the moment. The position of the trigrams is likened to a rainstorm that is about to break or a swollen river ready to gush forth – it is time for you to make the most of your own potential and of opportunities that are likely to appear.

姤

44. Kou

This hexagram is called To Meet, and combines the trigrams Ch'ien and Sun, heaven and wind.

Bear in mind that certain things are meant to be and others are either outside your control or totally unsuitable. There is the possibility of a beneficial meeting but do not be fooled by attention or flattery. You should think carefully before you change anything and be sure that the changes are appropriate.

45. Ts'ui

This hexagram is called To Collect, and combines the trigrams Tui and K'un, marsh and earth.

The emphasis in this hexagram is on order and harmony with the Tao, or the way of heaven. Study your environment carefully and give yourself time to reflect. Do not be too ambitious, and try to follow designs that are appropriate to your surroundings.

46. Sheng

This hexagram is called Rising Up, and combines the trigrams K'un and Sun, earth and wind.

The form of this hexagram is likened to seeds that have sprouted and flowered. It may take a long time for plans to materialize but patience will pay off. Everything seems to fall into place now so you should make the most of opportunities. Although this is a period of prosperity and growth it will not last forever, so be careful to remain on good terms with those who are working around you.

47. K'un

This hexagram is called To Surround and Wear Out, and combines the trigrams Tui and K'an, marsh and water.

There is a strong element of confinement in this hexagram and it is hard to see a way out. It offers very little encouragement and suggests that the best course is to be patient, assess your surroundings and find out what is really appropriate. The lines in this hexagram also warn against overspending; in the excitement of the moment it is easy to forget your future security.

48. Ching

This hexagram is called The Well, and combines the trigrams K'an and Sun, water and wind.

The underlying theme of this hexagram is our relationship with nature. We become weaker and less efficient by failing to take into account the rhythm and power of the natural world. Look at the shapes, forms and colours that surround you, and find a way of working in harmony with them.

49. Ko

This hexagram is called Change, and combines the trigrams Tui and Li, marsh and fire.

 This hexagram signifies the delicate balance between success and failure. The changes that you make may disappoint you because so much depends on a sound assessment of your needs and good timing. It may be time to change the old for the new, but you need to be sure that the time and the place are absolutely right.

51. Chen

This hexagram is called Shock, and the trigram Chen, thunder, appears twice.

It is said that the Chinese emperors came from thunder and that heaven and earth were moved by their strength. In this hexagram determination and strength have reached their peak, and it appears that nothing can stand in their way. Do not be alarmed by a sudden shock or unexpected event – it might be a positive time for change. Be alert and make the most of the potential in this hexagram.

50. Ting

This hexagram is called The Cooking Pot, and combines the trigrams Li and Sun, fire and wind.

This hexagram is likened to a meal that has been cooked to perfection over a flame. It takes careful preparation to produce food of a high standard just as it takes time and expertise to reorganize or redecorate. You need to plan carefully before embarking on a new project, and make sure that anyone helping you is suitable for the job.

52. Ken

This hexagram is called Resting, and the trigram Ken, mountain, appears twice.

A mountain is full of possibilities: it is sturdy, a place of peace and strength, and home to plants and animals. It is important to maintain this sense of reliability and determination in your life, and not be distracted by people or things that are not relevant to your plans. Follow your own instincts instead of being swayed by outside opinion.

53. Chien

This hexagram is called Gradual Development, and combines the trigrams Sun and Ken, wind and mountain.

The understanding that is gained through experience should not be underestimated. Enthusiasm is important, but without solid grounding you could easily stumble or make mistakes. If you are not experienced seek advice from someone who is; do not automatically assume that your designs or plans are the right ones, as the learning process can last for many years.

54. Kuei Mei

...ed Marrying the Younger Sister, and ...n and Tui, thunder and marsh.

...ive aspects of family ...ained in this hexagram. ...ying tensions or disagree- ...e sorted out. Identify where ...s likely to disagree. Try to cor- ...ey happen; if ignored they could ...le in the future.

55. Feng

This hexagram is called Prosperity, and combines the trigrams Chen and Li, thunder and fire.

This hexagram indicates productive and healthy authority – the earth is bright with fire, and thunder and lightning light up the sky. You have little to fear from anything or anyone, and nothing is likely to stand in your way at this time. However, do remember that times change; what appears to be a good idea one month may seem like a mistake the next. This process of change is the nature of the Tao, of which we are all part.

56. Lü

This hexagram is called The Traveller, and combines the trigrams Li and Ken, fire and mountain.

Movement and travel are at the heart of this hexagram. It is inevitable that at some point in your life you will have to let go of the familiar and enter strange territory. It takes time to adapt to a new environment and to understand its order. Do not force your particular tastes onto places or people where it is neither appreciated nor appropriate. Be tactful until you are sure of your environment.

57. Sun

This hexagram is called Gentle and Yielding, and the trigram Sun, wind, appears twice.

It is impossible to control the wind and hard to escape its effects; sometimes you have to give in to its penetrating power. This hexagram indicates that it is far more effective to use gentle and decisive powers of persuasion rather than force. You must understand who you are working with and what you hope to achieve.

58. Tui

This hexagram is called Happiness, and the trigram Tui, marsh, appears twice.

There is a strong element of pleasure and optimism in this hexagram. Everything is well catered for and content. A willingness to accept what is offered and consideration for others will help you to maintain this sense of well-being and satisfaction.

59. Huan

This hexagram is called Scattered, and combines the trigrams Sun and K'an, wind and water.

Just as the smooth surface of a lake can be disturbed by the wind, troubles that arrive unexpectedly can disturb your routine. This hexagram refers to a parting, but efforts will be made to return to a natural order. An unexpected change has many possibilities, so you should be open to new developments but beware of change that is forced on you or anyone else.

60. Chieh

This hexagram is called Limitations, and combines the trigrams K'an and Tui, water and marsh.

The mismanagement of water can result in drought or flood and its flow must be reasonably controlled. This hexagram indicates, similarly, that our lives must also be controlled and our resources neither underused nor overused. Do not be too hard on yourself since it is helpful to have space to relax in and luxuries to enjoy. In contrast, you should not be too indulgent or frivolous; you should regulate yourself and find a balance that suits your life.

中孚

61. Chung Fu

This hexagram is called Inner Confidence, and combines the trigrams Sun and Tui, wind and marsh.

There is an air of confidence here, a belief that everything will succeed and flow according to the Tao. You must find a balance between your emotional needs and the demands of everyday life. When you make this assessment make sure you do not forget others who come into contact with you. Have confidence in yourself and also in what you do.

小过

62. Hsiao Kuo

This hexagram is called Minor Problems, and combines the trigrams Chen and Ken, thunder and mountain.

Since this hexagram is more yin than yang it indicates a time of uncertainty and minor mistakes. There is an air of confusion but difficulties can be overcome and mistakes corrected. Do not assume that you are right or that your choice is necessarily the right choice. Everything is an experience; you can contribute something but you can also learn something, so proceed with moderation.

既济

63. Chi Chi

This hexagram is called Already Done, and combines the trigrams K'an and Li, water and fire.

This hexagram indicates that fire and water can be productive when they are used effectively. Similarly, it is possible to find a satisfactory way of working and a successful end, whatever the circumstances. But when you have completed a project do not sit back and assume that your work is finished. Although this hexagram is called Already Done, it also indicates that change is part of life's way, so be prepared for this. A new challenge may lie ahead.

未济

64. Wei Chi

This hexagram is called Not Yet Done, and combines the trigrams Li and K'an, fire and water.

This hexagram signifies that change is on the way and there may be a struggle ahead to achieve what you want. Be attentive and cautious; do not force your plans on anyone and do not rush ahead. Co-operation and patience are the key to success but do not assume that everything will work out as you planned.

Ring Two: The Directions

The directions fall into two categories: Western Life (shaded red on the dial) and Eastern Life (shaded gold on the dial). You will know from your personal Pa Tzu compass whether you are Eastern Life or Western Life, so you will be able to interpret the direction for which you are taking a reading in relation to your lucky and unlucky directions.

For example, if your Pa Tzu compass number is one and the direction of your reading is east, this direction is likely to bring you good fortune (so if you are taking a reading for the position of your desk this means you are likely to have a prosperous career). However, if the reading falls into one of your unlucky directions this is not necessarily a bad sign; if you obtain positive interpretations from the other rings you can find ways of compensating for this.

Ring Three: The Elements

Compare the element from this ring with your personal element from the Pa Tzu compass. Look for your combination in the table below to find out whether you have a positive or negative reading. For example, earth and metal are a positive combination since earth produces metal. If you have a positive reading you can continue onto the next ring. If you have a negative reading you should try another direction or follow the advice below on how to improve your reading.

Positive	Negative
wood produces fire	wood destroys earth
fire produces earth	earth destroys water
earth produces metal	water destroys fire
metal produces water	fire destroys metal
water produces wood	metal destroys wood

Element	Associated Colour	Suggested Improvements
wood	green	Introduce more plants, wooden features or objects made from wood, or wooden products, such as paper.
fire	red	Introduce more warm colours, fabrics, light or heating.
earth	yellow	Introduce more plants or earthy colours in paint and fabrics.
metal	white	Introduce metallic objects such as vases, candlesticks or furniture.
water	black	Introduce water itself or objects that have a yin quality, such as soft fabrics and subdued lighting.

ABOVE *Table of suggested improvements. If your reading is negative you can introduce colours and objects that correspond positively with your personal element.*

LEFT *Table showing the positive and negative combinations between the five elements.*

If both the elements are the same, for example wood and wood, refer to the table to find out which elements combine positively with wood, in this case fire and water. To improve your reading you should try to introduce colours or objects into your surroundings that are associated with either of these elements (*see table of suggested improvements*).

If you have a negative combination, for example your personal Pa Tzu element is earth and your *Feng Shui Kit* compass element is water, you can improve this combination. Look down the positive column to find an element that combines well with your personal Pa Tzu element. In this case earth produces metal, and fire produces earth, so you should try to introduce colours and objects associated with metal or fire (*see table of suggested improvements*).

Rings Four and Seven: Yin and Yang

These two rings are related to rings five and eight, as each of the twelve animals are linked to either yin or yang. At this stage your personal Chinese animal sign on the outer dial of the compass should be lined up with your main reading.

Compare the yin or yang reading on ring four with the yin or yang reading on ring seven. If one is yin and the other yang it is a positive reading since there is a dynamic interaction between the two forces. However, if both are yin or both are yang the reading is not as good, although you can compensate by increasing the yin or yang of the area as needed. For example, if you discover two yang readings you need to soften the colours and contours of the room to increase yin. You could also introduce water into the room. If both readings are yin you can increase the amount of yang by adding strong, bright colours. Fire and heat are also sources of yang.

If you discover two or more negative combinations in your reading it is advisable to try a new direction, although this may not always be possible. If this is the case, there are a number of things you can do to improve the feng shui of a room, such as hanging the pa kua mirror provided in this kit to deflect unlucky forces (*see page 70*), or adding plants, wind chimes or lamps to disperse malign forces and encourage ch'i.

Rings Five and Eight: The Twelve Animals

Compare your personal animal sign on ring eight with the animal sign that appears on ring five of the inner dial of the compass. The following interpretations overleaf on pages 46–69 reveal the compatibility between the different animal signs; remember that each reading should be interpreted in your own way, according to your character and circumstances.

For ease of reference, the illustrations of the twelve animals that appear on the inner dial of your *Feng Shui Kit* compass are also included on the following pages along with their own set of interpretations. The instructions for ring six follow on page 70.

RAT

RAT AND RAT

This seems to be a good match but dissatisfaction may set in after the initial excitement of change or the enthusiasm of facing a new challenge fades. You should focus on interesting objects and colours to maintain interest, and do not give up as soon as doubts set in.

RAT AND OX

This is a positive blend of steadiness, reliability and excitement, although at times the liveliness associated with the Rat could be overwhelming for the more sedate Ox. When you make plans you must remember to allow for your independence and your need for privacy.

RAT AND TIGER

There is a certain amount of risk in this combination, but this is also a challenging and stimulating match that could prove to be very exciting in the future. With a little time and understanding, any decisions that you make now could become a permanent feature.

RAT AND RABBIT

These signs are very different so it may be hard to find a balance between tranquillity and harmony, and colour and excitement. With a little effort these differences can be combined to good and long-lasting effect.

RAT AND DRAGON

Take a risk with stimulating and adventurous plans and combine them with attention to detail and thought for the future. This subtle partnership could produce exciting and fascinating results.

RAT AND SNAKE

There is a clash here between the desire for immediate action and the desire to use as little effort as possible. However, do not be frightened to make the most of opportunities that come your way as the outcome is likely to be positive.

RAT AND HORSE

This combination presents a conflict between hastily made decisions and the practical consequences of these decisions. Consideration and patience will improve the situation.

RAT AND RAM

It is hard to find a balance in this combination between the imaginative and the serviceable, and your creative impulses may be stifled by criticism. In order to maintain a sense of balance you should pursue your ideas and dreams but combine them with a practical outlook.

RAT AND MONKEY

There is a sense of complication and competitiveness here which you may enjoy. Alongside the dynamism in this combination, there is also instability. What you do may not be appreciated so you need to cultivate patience and trust.

RAT AND ROOSTER

Do not lose sight of your plans by becoming too critical or extravagant. You should try to work beyond the superficial to create a harmonious and well organized environment.

RAT AND DOG

An intimate atmosphere is created by this partnership. Your plans should focus on creating a secure environment that encourages not only trust, but also confidentiality.

RAT AND PIG

This is an exciting combination that is likely to bring enjoyment into your life. You take delight in being surrounded by the good things in life, and with the right amount of sensitivity your decisions should give you great pleasure.

OX

OX AND RAT

This is a positive blend of steadiness, reliability and excitement, although at times the liveliness associated with the Rat could be overwhelming for the more sedate Ox. When you make plans you must remember to allow for your independence and your need for privacy.

OX AND OX

There is a strong element of reliability and security in this combination and this is exactly what you need at this time. However, you should try to take a few risks with colour and design to avoid boredom setting in.

OX AND TIGER

One part of this combination wants to rise to a challenge and enjoys new designs or shapes, but the other needs reliability and familiarity. It may take a lot of effort to find a satisfying balance but with patience and adaptability this can be achieved. Use colour, texture, plants and flowers to create natural and interesting effects.

OX AND RABBIT

Once the initial feeling of hesitancy in this combination has been dealt with there are plenty of good opportunities in store for the future. However, the emphasis is very much on familiarity, reliabililty and a peaceful home life.

OX AND DRAGON

There is an inclination to make a decision on the spur of the moment but this is tempered by the need for patience and familiarity. This combination could prove to be an invigorating experience, although you may feel the need for a change of surroundings from time to time.

OX AND SNAKE

There is a combination of reflection and action here, and this makes for a fairly balanced match. You should make sure you plan for the future with an eye on comfort and security.

OX AND HORSE

There is a clash here between a need for peace and tranquillity and a desire for action and spur-of-the-moment decisions. It may be hard to adapt or come to terms with your circumstances, but try to make room for the romantic as well as the practical. Make your environment a place where you can find peace, but one that also welcomes others.

OX AND RAM

Creative skills and practical needs could blend well together here, although it is possible that imagination and flights of fancy could make it difficult to work practically with an eye for detail. Try to combine the idealistic with the realistic to achieve what you want.

OX AND MONKEY

This is a fine blend of originality and stability, a combination that impresses with both colour and style and at the same time provides comfortable surroundings.

OX AND ROOSTER

This combination indicates the need to create a comforting, peaceful and welcoming environment, but do not forget to add a splash of style.

OX AND DOG

You like to feel safe and secure, and this combination brings a depth and stability to your planning that should encourage relaxation and reliability.

OX AND PIG

This is a peaceful and pleasant combination, although there is a need for occasional colour and excitement which you must not ignore.

TIGER

TIGER AND RAT

There is a certain amount of risk here, but this is also a challenging combination that could prove to be very exciting. With time and understanding whatever you decide on now could become a permanent feature.

TIGER AND OX

One part of this combination wants to rise to a challenge and enjoys new designs or shapes, but the other needs reliability and familiarity. It may take a lot of effort to find a satisfying balance but with patience and adaptability this can be achieved. Use colour, texture, plants and flowers to create natural and interesting effects.

TIGER AND TIGER

The emphasis here is on independence and action but be careful not to push it too far. You need your privacy and freedom, and therefore an environment that encourages you to relax and calm down would be very useful. You need to find a balance between stimulation and reflection.

TIGER AND RABBIT

This blend should work well as long as you create a comfortable and secure environment that still provides a sense of privacy and freedom. However, it will fail if your plans are too predictable or too adventurous.

TIGER AND DRAGON

Energy and excitement drive you on and you will soon become tired of predictable or dull surroundings. Stop to think before you overspend on luxurious items or expensive designs.

TIGER AND SNAKE

There might be too much vitality and risk in this combination; on the one hand there is a desire for surroundings that are peaceful and reflective, and on the other a need for action and colour. The solution may be to create two separate areas, one that is vibrant and one that is relaxing.

TIGER AND HORSE

Enthusiasm and excitement are likely to rule your decisions, but try not to forget others when you make plans since their suggestions and participation could be beneficial. This is a combination that is bustling with life and possibilities.

TIGER AND RAM

These two complement each other well and your level of enthusiasm is high, but make sure you keep a watchful eye on your spending.

TIGER AND MONKEY

There is a certain amount of uncertainty and confusion here. This could be smoothed out with a little less criticism and more shared support.

TIGER AND ROOSTER

The emphasis here is on creating a good impression at first sight, but it may be difficult to find something that will satisfy in the long-term. Do not make decisions too quickly, and give yourself time for reflection before you act.

TIGER AND DOG

This is a union that is full of possibilities but do not be too idealistic; you need a certain amount of common sense in your planning.

TIGER AND PIG

Confidence and individuality are strong elements here. It is important that you do not feel trapped by your surroundings.

RABBIT

RABBIT AND RAT

These signs are very different, so it may be hard to find a balance between the need for something that is tranquil and harmonious, and the need for something that is colourful and exciting. With a little effort these differences can be combined to good and long-lasting effect.

RABBIT AND OX

Once the initial feeling of hesitancy in this combination has been dealt with there are plenty of good opportunities in store. However, the emphasis is very much on familiarity, reliabililty and a peaceful home life. Use natural colours, textures, and familiar objects to create a homely atmosphere

RABBIT AND TIGER

This blend should work well as long as you create a comfortable and secure environment that at the same time provides a sense of privacy and freedom. However, it will fail if your plans are too predictable or too adventurous – you need to find a balance between the two.

RABBIT AND RABBIT

You need to feel safe and secure. This is not a dynamic combination but it is a peaceful one, so you should create a quiet place that encourages harmony through restful designs and colours.

RABBIT AND DRAGON

It is difficult to create a suitable atmosphere since there is a sharp contrast here between dynamism and orderliness. Concessions may have to be made in both directions.

RABBIT AND SNAKE

Focus on surroundings that give you a feeling of security and peace but are also pleasing to the eye. You have a love of beautiful objects and have met the right match in this combination.

RABBIT AND HORSE

Confidence and enthusiasm will help to overcome any hesitations that may arise from this combination, but you need to beware of being too confident or selfish.

RABBIT AND RAM

You need to feel secure and at peace in your surroundings. This partnership provides this security and at the same time allows for creative input and freedom of expression.

RABBIT AND MONKEY

You have a sound sense of intuition which could be put to good effect here. Intimacy and reliability are strong elements in this partnership, although you can afford to take the occasional risk.

RABBIT AND ROOSTER

There is a clash here between a need to impress and a desire for comfort and privacy. Creating vibrant and colourful surroundings is appealing, but do not forget that you also need a place to relax and unwind.

RABBIT AND DOG

You feel protective about your home and the atmosphere it creates, so this is a good combination if you are deciding on a quiet personal area.

RABBIT AND PIG

Privacy and peace suit your character and this is a restful and harmonious combination. You like to feel at ease with the furniture and colours around you, although a sudden burst of colour or an unusual design would add a lively dimension to your surroundings.

DRAGON

DRAGON AND RAT

Take a risk with stimulating and adventurous plans and combine them with attention to detail and thought for the future. This subtle partnership could produce exciting and fascinating results if given the opportunity.

DRAGON AND OX

There is an inclination to make a decision on the spur of the moment but this is tempered by the need for patience and familiarity. This combination could prove to be an invigorating experience, although you may feel the need for a change of surroundings from time to time.

DRAGON AND TIGER

Energy and excitement drive you on and you will soon become tired of predictable or dull surroundings. You are likely to enjoy unusual or innovative designs but stop to think before you overspend on luxurious items or expensive decorations.

DRAGON AND RABBIT

It is difficult to create a suitable atmosphere since there is a sharp contrast here between dynamism and orderliness. Concessions may have to be made in both directions.

DRAGON AND DRAGON

You are attracted to bright colours, exciting designs and unusual settings, and you enjoy impressing others with your style. This is a lively and positive blend that is full of bright ideas, but remember that others can offer you valuable advice.

DRAGON AND SNAKE

Allow a certain style and flair into your plans as long as it does not upset your rhythm and comforts. It is possible to be surrounded by all the objects you like and still impress others with lively form and colour.

DRAGON AND HORSE

Try not to let your enthusiasm or personal needs rule your decisions too much. Privacy is important to you, as is the need for your work to be admired.

DRAGON AND RAM

In this combination there is a temptation to let your imagination run free with design and colour, but it may not always please others. You should try to be more open to advice.

DRAGON AND MONKEY

This is an exciting combination that encourages confidence and success. There is an emphasis on the daring, the unusual and the fascinating.

DRAGON AND ROOSTER

This combination has plenty of flair, colour and excitement. You prefer a lively approach to a subtle one, and this particular combination is suited to the side of your character that enjoys entertainment and performance.

DRAGON AND DOG

It is hard for these two signs to relate to each other; on the one hand there is a search for comfort and on the other there is a need to be extravagant. You should create two areas, one that is bustling with life and attracts attention and another that is secure and calm.

DRAGON AND PIG

There are exciting possibilities here, although you may find it hard to make a final decision on a colour scheme or piece of furniture. There is scope for an unusual design or colour combination, so make the most of the opportunity.

SNAKE

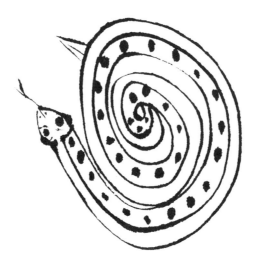

SNAKE AND RAT

There is a clash here between the desire for immediate action and the desire to use as little effort as possible. However, do not be frightened to make the most of opportunities that come your way as the outcome is likely to be positive.

SNAKE AND OX

This is a combination of reflection and action. You should make sure you plan for the future with an eye on comfort and security.

SNAKE AND RABBIT

Focus on surroundings that give you a feeling of security and peace but are also pleasing to the eye. You have a love of beautiful objects and have met the right match in this combination. You are likely to have good taste, so take advantage of this and make the most of fabrics, textures and colours.

SNAKE AND DRAGON

Allow a certain style and flair into your plans as long as it does not upset your rhythm and home comforts. It is possible to be surrounded by all the objects you like and still impress others with lively form and colour.

SNAKE AND TIGER

There might be too much vitality and risk in this combination; on the one hand there is a desire for surroundings that are peaceful and reflective, and on the other a need for action and colour. The solution may be to create two separate areas, one that is vibrant and one that is relaxing.

SNAKE AND SNAKE

There is a great sense of amusement and pleasure in this combination but it could burn itself out. Try to maintain your individual style, and do not crowd yourself.

SNAKE AND HORSE

There are plenty of exciting and positive possibilities in this combination. You have a need to express yourself in your surroundings, but try not to reject suggestions from others.

SNAKE AND RAM

There is a strong love of art and harmony here. Your efforts should focus on creating a pleasing and imaginative environment, but you should try to avoid disagreements with others along the way.

SNAKE AND MONKEY

This is a stimulating and intelligent combination, especially suited to the work place. Although you are able to assess situations quickly and shrewdly, you should also give yourself time to consider decisions carefully. If you have to move in a rush you will be able to adapt with ease.

SNAKE AND ROOSTER

The emphasis in this combination is on elegance and style. Whatever appeals to your good sense of taste, colour and design will work well here.

SNAKE AND DOG

This partnership has the potential to be quite effective, and combines a home-loving, reliable outlook with a sense of adventure.

SNAKE AND PIG

On the surface this does not appear to be a comfortable combination, but with time it could become stimulating and challenging. There is a shared appreciation of visually pleasing objects which is combined with attention to detail.

HORSE

HORSE AND RAT

This combination presents a conflict between hastily made decisions and the practical consequences of these decisions. Consideration and patience will improve the situation.

HORSE AND OX

There is a clash here between the need for peace and tranquillity and a desire for action and spur-of-the-moment decisions. It may be hard to adapt or come to terms with your circumstances, but try to make room for the romantic as well as the practical. Make your environment a place where you can find peace, but make sure that it is also welcoming to others.

HORSE AND TIGER

Enthusiasm and excitement are likely to rule your decisions, but try not to forget others when you make plans since their suggestions and participation could be beneficial. This is a combination that is bustling with life and it offers many interesting and stimulating possibilities.

HORSE AND RABBIT

Confidence and enthusiasm will help to overcome any hesitations that may arise from this combination, but you need to beware of being too confident or selfish.

HORSE AND DRAGON

Try not to let your enthusiasm or personal needs rule your decisions too much. Privacy is important to you, as is the need for your work to be admired.

HORSE AND SNAKE

There are plenty of positive and exciting possibilities in this combination. You have a need to express yourself in your surroundings, but try not to reject suggestions from others.

HORSE AND HORSE

There is a strong level of excitement and dynamism in this partnership. However, you should think carefully before you make decisions in order to avoid disappointment in the future.

HORSE AND RAM

This is a good combination that suits your sense of fun, your willingness to deal with the unexpected and your dislike of the mundane. There are plenty of exciting opportunities here.

HORSE AND MONKEY

There is a conflict here between a sensible course of action and one that is made on the spur of the moment. In order to find a balance let your ideas flow freely and use your imagination, but give yourself time to assess what is happening and consider the outcome.

HORSE AND ROOSTER

The desire to impress is strong, as is a sensitivity to your surroundings, but you need more patience. You may find that it is not long before you feel the need for a change.

HORSE AND DOG

There is a strong element of privacy and independence in this combination. You should follow your instincts rather than trying to impress others.

HORSE AND PIG

This is an easy and comfortable combination but it could require a good deal of time and effort to maintain. Do not be surprised if you feel the need for a change after a while.

RAM

RAM AND RAT

It is hard to find a balance here between the imaginative and the serviceable, and your creative impulses may be stifled by criticism. In order to maintain a sense of balance you should pursue your ideas and dreams but combine them with a practical outlook.

RAM AND OX

Creative skills and practical needs could blend well together here, although it is possible that imagination and flights of fancy could make it difficult to work practically with an eye for detail. Try to combine the idealistic with the realistic to achieve what you want.

RAM AND TIGER

These two complement each other well and your level of enthusiasm is high. However, you must make sure you keep a watchful eye on your spending. While you have a love of fine objects and attractive surroundings, from time to time you need to experience a change of scene.

RAM AND RABBIT

You need to feel secure and at peace in your surroundings. This partnership provides this security and at the same time allows for creative input.

RAM AND DRAGON

In this combination there is a temptation to let your imagination run free with design and colour, but it may not always please others. You should try to be more open to advice.

RAM AND SNAKE

There is a strong love of art and harmony in this combination. Your efforts should focus on creating a pleasing and imaginative environment, but try to avoid disagreements with others along the way.

RAM AND HORSE

This is a good combination that suits your sense of fun, your willingness to deal with the unexpected and your dislike of the mundane. There are plenty of exciting opportunities here.

RAM AND RAM

You have a strong love of art and unusual styles appeal to you, but do not disregard your financial limitations in pursuit of beauty.

RAM AND MONKEY

Imagination and intelligence work well together here, but there is also a strong element of fun. There is a sense of immediacy but you may become bored or disillusioned quickly. Be attentive to your surroundings and be prepared for changes and alterations in order to maintain interest.

RAM AND ROOSTER

This is a good combination if you are planning to entertain, but ultimately it will be hard to establish a sense of harmony. Give yourself time to combine sensitivity and understanding with creativity and daring designs.

RAM AND DOG

There is a conflict here between common sense and idealism, and it may be hard to make a decision due to doubts and anxieties. Your environment should be comfortable, safe and reassuring, but do not forget that a creative and fresh input could add a positive dimension.

RAM AND PIG

These two signs combine harmony as well as a shared sense of beauty. You enjoy a peaceful and creative environment, but make sure you keep a watchful eye on your finances.

MONKEY

MONKEY AND RAT

There is a sense of complication and competitiveness here which you may enjoy. Alongside the dynamism in this combination, there is also instability. What you do may not be appreciated so you need to cultivate patience and trust.

MONKEY AND OX

This is a fine blend of originality and stability, a combination that impresses with both colour and style and at the same time provides comfortable surroundings.

MONKEY AND TIGER

There is a certain amount of uncertainty and confusion here. This could be smoothed out with a little less criticism and more shared support.

MONKEY AND RABBIT

You have a sound sense of intuition which could be put to good effect here. Intimacy and reliability are strong elements in this partnership, although you can afford to take the occasional risk.

MONKEY AND DRAGON

This is an exciting combination that encourages confidence and success. There is an emphasis on the daring, the unusual and the fascinating.

MONKEY AND SNAKE

This is a stimulating and intelligent combination, especially suited to the work place. Although you are able to assess situations quickly and shrewdly, you should also give yourself time to consider decisions carefully. If you have to move in a rush you will be able to adapt with ease.

MONKEY AND HORSE

There is a conflict here between a sensible course of action and one that is made on the spur of the moment. In order to find a balance let your ideas flow freely and use your imagination, but give yourself time to assess what is happening and consider the outcome.

MONKEY AND RAM

Imagination and intelligence work well together here, but there is also a strong element of fun. There is a sense of immediacy but you may become bored or disillusioned quickly. Be attentive to your surroundings and be prepared for changes and alterations in order to maintain interest.

MONKEY AND MONKEY

This is an intelligent and stimulating partnership that should not only be easy to live with, but should also improve with time.

MONKEY AND ROOSTER

There is uncertainty ahead, so reliability and consideration are particularly important here; think very carefully before you make any decisions. You need an environment that is both stimulating and inviting to others.

MONKEY AND DOG

There is a combination of idealism and cynicism here that should be handled very carefully. You need to create an environment that contains stimulating objects and colours but is also reassuring and traditional.

MONKEY AND PIG

This combination has a great deal of potential, and with careful handling and honest evaluation this will prove to be a good match that is both sensitive and appealing.

ROOSTER

ROOSTER AND RAT

Do not lose sight of your plans by becoming too critical or too extravagant. You should try to work beyond the superficial to create a harmonious and well organized environment.

ROOSTER AND OX

This combination indicates the need to create a comforting, peaceful and welcoming environment, but do not forget to add a splash of style and allow for your sense of creativity.

ROOSTER AND TIGER

The emphasis here is on creating a good impression at first sight, but it may be difficult to find something that will satisfy in the long-term. Do not make decisions too quickly, and give yourself time for reflection before you act.

ROOSTER AND RABBIT

There is a clash in this combination between a need to impress and a desire for privacy and comfort. Creating vibrant and colourful surroundings is appealing, but do not forget that you also need a place where you can relax and unwind.

ROOSTER AND DRAGON

This combination has plenty of flair, colour and excitement. You prefer a lively approach to a subtle one, and this particular combination suits the side of your character that enjoys performance.

ROOSTER AND SNAKE

The emphasis in this combination is on elegance and style. Whatever appeals to your good sense of taste, colour and design will work well here.

ROOSTER AND HORSE

The desire to impress is particularly strong in this combination, as is a sensitivity to your surroundings. However, you need more patience, and you may find that it is not long before you feel the need for a change.

ROOSTER AND RAM

This is a good combination if you are planning to entertain, but it will be hard to establish a sense of harmony. These two signs will work well together if you take the time to combine sensitivity and understanding with creativity and daring designs.

ROOSTER AND MONKEY

There is uncertainty ahead, so reliability and consideration are particularly important here; think very carefully before you make any decisions. You need an environment that is both stimulating and inviting to others.

ROOSTER AND ROOSTER

Time may be taken up finding faults with superficial points but underneath there is a good appreciation of style and individuality. In your enthusiasm for choosing furniture or home decorations make sure you keep an eye on your finances.

ROOSTER AND DOG

Both of these signs have a critical and sensitive edge, but you need to beware of being too critical in your choices or you will lose a sense of satisfaction. Decoration and style are particularly important in this match, but make sure that you do not overspend.

ROOSTER AND PIG

This partnership combines a flair for style with an understanding of practical needs. You are likely to feel most at home in a relaxed and easygoing atmosphere.

DOG

DOG AND RAT

A warm and intimate atmosphere is created by this partnership. Your plans should focus on creating an environment that encourages not only trust, but also confidentiality.

DOG AND OX

You like to feel safe and secure, and this match brings a depth and stability to your planning. You should create surroundings that encourage relaxation, but do not forget to pay attention to detail.

DOG AND TIGER

This is a union that is full of possibilities but do not be too idealistic; you need a certain amount of common sense in your planning.

DOG AND RABBIT

You feel protective about your home and the atmosphere it creates, so this is a good combination for a quiet personal area. You are attached to, and affected by, your surroundings so choose colours and objects you can easily live with.

DOG AND DRAGON

It is hard for these two signs to relate to each other; on the one hand there is a search for comfort and on the other there is a need to be extravagant. You should create two areas, one that is bustling with life and attracts attention and another that is secure and calm.

DOG AND SNAKE

This partnership has the potential to be quite effective, and combines a home-loving, reliable outlook with a sense of adventure.

DOG AND HORSE

There is a strong element of privacy and independence in this combination. You should follow your instincts rather than trying to impress others.

DOG AND RAM

There is a conflict here between common sense and idealism, and it may be hard to make a decision due to doubts and anxieties. Your environment should be comfortable, safe and reassuring, but do not forget that a creative and fresh input could add a positive dimension.

DOG AND MONKEY

There is a combination of idealism and cynicism here that needs to be handled very carefully. You need to create an environment that contains stimulating objects and colours but is also reassuring and traditional.

DOG AND ROOSTER

Both of these signs have a critical and sensitive edge, but you need to beware of being too critical in your choices or you will lose a sense of satisfaction. Decoration and style are important in this match, but make sure that you do not overspend.

DOG AND DOG

Planning for the security and comfort of the family is important in this combination. You should feel content in a reliable and familiar atmosphere, and are likely to prosper in safe and protected place.

DOG AND PIG

An element of fun and colour combines well with something comfortable and reliable in this partnership. However, in order to make the most of life you need to feel secure and reassured.

PIG

PIG AND RAT

This is an exciting match that is likely to bring you enjoyment. You take delight in being surrounded by the good things in life, and with sensitivity your decisions should give you great pleasure.

PIG AND OX

This is a peaceful and pleasant combination with an air of reliability and security about it. However, there is a need for occasional excitement and a splash of colour which you must not ignore.

PIG AND TIGER

Confidence and individuality are strong elements here. It is important that you do not feel trapped by your surroundings. There is a shared enjoyment of luxurious items and interesting designs, but also a need for private space.

PIG AND RABBIT

Privacy and peace suit your character and this is a restful and harmonious combination. You like to feel at ease with the furniture and colours around you, although a sudden burst of colour or an unusual design would add a lively dimension to your surroundings.

PIG AND DRAGON

There are exciting possibilities here, although it may be hard to make a final decision on a colour scheme or piece of furniture. There is scope for an unusual design or colour combination.

PIG AND SNAKE

On the surface this does not appear to be a comfortable combination, but with time it could become stimulating and challenging.

PIG AND HORSE

This is an easy and comfortable combination but it could require a good deal of time and effort to maintain. Do not be surprised if you feel the need for change after a while.

PIG AND RAM

These two signs combine harmony as well as a shared sense of beauty, so they make for a good match. You enjoy a peaceful and creative environment, but make sure you keep a watchful eye on

your finances since you may find yourself tempted by unusual and expensive items.

PIG AND MONKEY

This combination has a great deal of potential, and with careful handling and honest evaluation this will prove to be a good match that is both sensitive and appealing.

PIG AND ROOSTER

This partnership combines a flair for style with an understanding of practical needs. You are likely to feel most at home in a relaxed and easygoing atmosphere.

PIG AND DOG

An element of fun and colour combines well with something comfortable and reliable in this partnership. However, in order to make the most of life you need to feel secure and reassured.

PIG AND PIG

This is a well-matched pair and there are plenty of exciting possibilities here. You like being surrounded by objects and colours that are easy to live with, bright and pleasing to the eye.

Ring Six: The Compass Degrees

The compass degrees are used on feng shui compasses to give an accurate siting. Each degree is marked by a line on ring six, and the degrees are further divided into groups of ten. For example, if your reading is in the north-west direction it corresponds to water, yin, the Pig and 300°–330°. This is one of your lucky directions if your Pa Tzu compass belongs to the Western Life category. You can be more specific about the siting by finding out exactly which degree lies under the nylon thread.

If you are planning to decorate several rooms or build a house then it would be useful to take a note of the degrees at which your lucky and unlucky directions lie. Each time you take a new reading, make a note of the compass degrees so that you will then have an immediate reference for a later date.

The Pa Kua Mirror

Mirrors are used to deflect malign forces or spirits, such as bad luck, corruption or ill health. In many instances they are the most effective way to hasten the pace of slow-moving ch'i, to free blocked ch'i or to regulate ch'i that may be running through your house or garden too quickly. A mirror can be placed either inside or outside an office or house to counteract a negative reading and improve the feng shui of the area.

One of the most common places to hang a mirror is above the front door, but they are also often positioned in a hallway facing the front door or on a landing at the top of a flight of stairs. If one of the rooms in your house faces an unlucky feature outside, such as a sharp bend in the road or a gap between two buildings, then a mirror can be placed on a wall facing this feature in order to deflect the unlucky forces.

A traditional pa kua mirror. The god of the north is one of many thought to help ward off unlucky spirits.

Mirrors specially designed for this purpose are known as *pa kua*. They are usually small and round, and set in wood. The most simple pa kua has the eight trigrams drawn around the mirror. On more elaborate models, a god is pictured with the mirror to help deflect any malign influences. The traditional pa kua pictured to the left shows the god of the north; others might include the vivid and fearsome god of war.

The order of the trigrams that appear around *The Feng Shui Kit* pa kua mirror follow the Former Heaven Sequence, which is the alternative sequence to that used on *The Feng Shui Kit* compass and also in the Pa Tzu compass system. We have followed the Former Heaven Sequence as this is traditionally used on pa kua mirrors. When you are reading the lines of each trigram the upper line is on the outside and the lower line is on the inside. You can position the simple pa kua mirror provided in this kit where you feel it will be most useful and lucky for you. (Pa kua mirrors can also be bought at most Chinese supermarkets.)

Although the colourful pa kua mirror looks impressive, other mirrors may also be used to deflect misfortune. For some people, even a reflective piece of metal will satisfy the demands of feng shui; it could be a polished wok or pan, or a piece of polished metal from a tin or a chest.

In the following chapters there is specific advice on where to put the pa kua mirror to improve your reading or generally enhance the feng shui of an area, as well as other helpful suggestions on how to deal with unlucky features.

The Feng Shui Ruler

The feng shui ruler is used to measure the height of desks, chairs, tables and other furniture, as well as any features on or outside a building, and is often used in the work place. There are different categories of reading on the ruler – some imply good luck and others indicate loss or the possibility of a financial setback. The ruler is a traditional tool that is used by a feng shui expert to add another dimension to the compass reading, although the compass is still the main source for discovering auspicious directions.

You will notice that there are divisions along each side of *The Feng Shui Kit* compass edge. These divisions represent the ruler categories, and they have been simplified and adapted from the traditional feng shui ruler pictured below.

The category names are printed on the sheet of stickers included with this kit. The names of the outdoor categories are printed in gold on a red background, and the names of the indoor ones are printed in red with a gold background. The stickers should be positioned in the allocated spaces contained within the divisions – refer to the chart on the next page for the corresponding number to each category. The arrows marked on two corners of the compass indicate the starting point for each group of measurements.

The traditional feng shui ruler, as used by feng shui masters. The Chinese characters running along the centre of the ruler denote the categories for indoor and outdoor measurements.

Feng Shui Ruler Measurements

Categories for Outdoor Measurements

1 一 **Wealth** indicates increased earnings or an unexpected windfall.

2 二 **Disease** indicates the possibility of sickness or minor infections.

3 三 **Departure** indicates departure from a work place, home or person.

4 四 **Reason** indicates well thought-out discussion, plans and actions.

5 五 **Promotion** indicates success and good fortune at work.

6 六 **Loss** indicates the loss of material possessions.

7 七 **Harm** indicates damage to an object or the possibility of an accident.

8 八 **Capital** indicates successful investment and financial stability.

Categories for Indoor Measurements

1 一 **Harm** indicates the possibility of minor accidents or illness.

2 二 **Prosperity** indicates good fortune and general well-being.

3 三 **Distress** indicates worry or concern over domestic or career matters.

4 四 **Reason** indicates well thought-out discussion, plans and actions.

5 五 **Career** indicates the chance of promotion or success at work.

6 六 **Parting** indicates losing touch with a person or group of people.

7 七 **Growth** indicates business expansion or positive developments at work or at home.

8 八 **Separation** indicates losing contact with a person or a place.

9 九 **Wealth** indicates increased earnings or an unexpected windfall.

10 十 **Children** indicates a fruitful and happy family life.

The eight divisions that appear on two sides of *The Feng Shui Kit* compass are used to measure outdoor measurements, such as walls, garden fences and the height of windows. They begin with a category known as *wealth* and end with *capital*; the eight categories are then repeated until the required height is measured. You will find that the scale continues along the edge of the second side (there are four divisions along each of the two sides). On most occasions, you will need to rotate the compass onto this side to continue your measurement, noting the position of the end of the scale so that you can reposition the compass at this point.

The ten divisions that appear on the other two sides of the compass (five on each side) are used to measure the height of furniture or architectural features inside the house. They begin with the category *harm* and end with *children*; the ten categories are then repeated until the required height is measured.

When you have measured your object you will need to refer to the chart on the left to discover what your measurement means. The interpretations for each of the outdoor and indoor categories reveal whether the measurement you have taken is a fortunate one, or whether it indicates the possibility of misfortune, at home or at work. Every reading you take should be interpreted according to your particular situation.

Conflicting Readings

If you are taking a reading with *The Feng Shui Kit* compass or ruler for a building, room or object that is shared by another person or group of people then you may need to take several readings, one for each person concerned. If some readings are lucky and others are unlucky, one solution would be to try a new direction. However, this may not always be possible, so an alternative way to remedy the situation would be to introduce certain colours or objects to improve the unlucky readings (*see page 44*).

The introduction of a lamp or wall light, a tree, or a vase of flowers may provide the added dimension that you are looking for, as well as improving the flow of ch'i. The guidelines in the following chapter will help you with planning and design, both inside and outside your home.

CHAPTER FOUR

FENG SHUI AT HOME

Health

Your *Feng Shui Kit* compass, ruler and pa kua mirror can be easily used inside or outside the home. You can use the compass to assess the direction of your house, of individual rooms, or directions within the rooms themselves. You can use the ruler to measure the height of furniture, windows, doors, fences or other features, and the pa kua mirror can be hung inside or outside your house to improve your feng shui reading. But in order to make the most of the feng shui potential of your home you will also need to be familiar with the general principles which apply to the flow of ch'i and the arrangement of furniture, buildings and architectural features. This chapter introduces you to the feng shui principles which apply to the location of a house, its proportions and its interior design. Remember that in addition to these guidelines, you can use your *Feng Shui Kit* compass to take a *personal* reading for anything in your surroundings.

The Four Animal Spirits

The animals and forces at work in the natural features of the land are equally as important in the feng shui of the home. The positioning of a house and garden in relation to trees, water, quality of soil and light as well as neighbouring buildings can affect the prosperity and well-being of the people who live there.

According to the Chinese, the boundaries of the home are marked and guarded by four animal spirits.

The boundaries of the home are guarded by the four animal spirits.

These are represented by a Black Tortoise, a Red Bird, a White Tiger, and a Green Dragon.

These four creatures not only symbolize the animal kingdom but also represent north, south, east and west – the four quarters of the sky – and the four seasons. This particular formation marks the location of a classic feng shui site in the landscape. The Black Tortoise is seen in higher land and is the protector from harsh weather. The Green Dragon and White Tiger are seen in slightly lower hills or slopes and they are the guardians of the site; ideally the dragon should be slightly higher than the tiger in order to keep the hungry tiger at bay. The Red Bird, seen in the lowest hill or rise in the land, lies to the front of the house allowing good ch'i to flow over its back and circulate gently with the existing ch'i of the site.

Your Home and its Surroundings

Any building work should take into account the nature of these animal spirits. The Green Dragon and White Tiger are believed to guard the house and should be

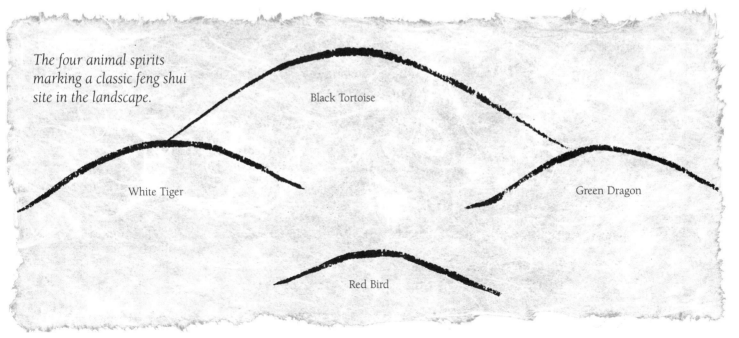

The four animal spirits marking a classic feng shui site in the landscape.

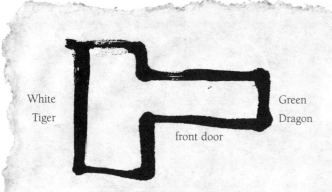

Extensions or additional floors on the side of the White Tiger make the building unbalanced. As a result, the White Tiger 'devours' the Green Dragon, and this could affect the health of the occupants.

The kitchen, main bedroom and living-room should be in the 'ankle' of this shoe-shaped house. A lamp, pond or tree in the garden would create a sense of balance, and trees or plants would also take the pressure away from the 'heel'.

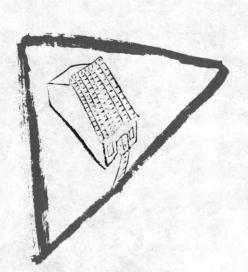

Triangular plots are generally unlucky unless they are terraced. A long, narrow house on such a site could cause domestic or health problems.

A large back garden acts as support and protection for the house. Square or rectangular plots of land make good feng shui sites.

If the house is shaped like a knife, the strength is in the handle and the weakness is in the blade. All the main rooms should be in the handle.

This house would be balanced by the addition of a tree or pond to create a rectangular shape.

Your house should be at least as high as the neighbouring houses, and the houses behind it should be slightly higher to offer protection.

To ensure the smooth flow of ch'i your house should not be sandwiched between higher buildings either to the side or to the front.

well-balanced. This co-ordination on either side of the house can be achieved if both sides of the house are similar in their proportions. If additional floors or extensions make one side much larger or wider than the other, one animal could become too powerful and difficult to control, which in turn could affect the health of the occupants.

If you live in a terraced or semi-detached house, or in an apartment, the same rules apply to the whole building. When you look at the block there should be a sense of balance and unity in its construction – one side or corner of the building should not look top-heavy or out of proportion with the rest. A building does not always have to be perfectly symmetrical, but there should be a sense of proportion not only in the building itself but also in relation to the features and architecture around it. In addition, the building should also have a greater width than depth to encourage stability; it is said that long thin houses could cause depression and respiratory problems. As well as increased width, houses or apartments with bay windows or curved brickwork on either side of the main entrance are believed to bring prosperity and respect to those living there.

As the Black Tortoise should be higher than the Red Bird, your back garden should be slightly higher than your front garden. If you only have a small plot of land at the back of your home this should be level to prevent ch'i rolling too quickly towards the house. The back garden should also be larger than the front to act as protection and support for those inside the house. Feng shui warns against front gardens that slope upwards from the front door, as this could cause family disagreements or financial loss.

The ideal shape for a building plot is a square piece of land, and the least auspicious is a triangular plot. If your house was originally built on a square or oblong plot but part of the land has been eroded, flooded or used for construction, the best advice is to try and

The wings of this house overwhelm the entrance and limit the flow of ch'i. Trees or light encourage ch'i into the house and a porch, wall or door would regulate the shape of the house.

Do not plant trees directly outside the front door; they have a strong yin nature and make it difficult for yang to enter.

Trees are a rich source of ch'i and provide a protective barrier between a house and a busy main road.

reclaim the land, or even the sides or corners, so that it is brought back into line. According to feng shui a weak corner or side to the land could cause health problems, ranging from stomach disorders and flu to an increase in accidents around the home. Buildings that do have jutting extensions or unusual shapes are often likened to objects such as knives or shoes, and their proportions can usually be regulated with simple additions such as a lamp, mirror or tree. Whenever possible, it is best to round off sharp edges and jutting corners to help ch'i flow over the edges.

In order for ch'i to circulate freely, and for yin and yang to maintain a balance, you should avoid water-logged land or sites that have been built on reclaimed disposal ground. This is based on the practical principle that the conditions of the site may cause ill health, damp or structural problems. The ideal soil is one that is well aerated, and neither too wet nor too dry.

In urban areas the buildings themselves should be planned according to a pattern, otherwise the flow of ch'i may disperse too easily or become blocked through irregular planning. This pattern does not have to be tightly regulated, but it should ensure that the buildings are not randomly scattered at different heights to one another.

For practical reasons, trees should not be planted too close to the house. Those with deep roots may undermine the foundations or tall trees may block the amount of light entering. Trees should not be planted directly outside the front door as they are a strong source of yin and will inhibit the amount of yang entering the house. However, when planted in positive feng shui positions trees can provide good protection against malign forces. They are used to maintain an environmental balance, and their healthy growth is a sign of rich ch'i in the earth. They should therefore be planted if the land is available, but they should not be too densely packed around a building. If your house is close to a busy road a screen of trees should be built to protect it from noise and fumes. Be careful not to let these trees grow higher than the house itself as, apart from blocking out the light, their yin nature could be overpowering.

Water is also a strong source of yin, and if you have a pond or pool in your garden, or a stream running through it, plants such as magnolia and osmanthus help to re-establish the balance between yin and yang. Try to avoid banyan trees or azaleas which may encourage further yin. It is believed that water attracts money and good ch'i can be drawn in from distant water by placing a pa kua mirror outside the house. However, if a stream is flowing too fast and cutting off a corner of the garden this could drain your finances, and the course of the stream should be altered or the flow slowed down with plants or rocks.

A fast-flowing stream can drain money away unless the flow is broken up by rocks and plants.

A mirror outside the house or in the hallway can attract good fortune from distant water.

A twisting path should lead to a pond that is situated close to a house to give an increased sense of distance.

Manhole covers should be hidden by pots containing herbs, flowers or shrubs to encourage ch'i.

Ch'i is lost quickly down wide driveways, particularly if the house is built at the top of a hill. Lamps at the door can help to control the flow of ch'i.

RIGHT An outside lamp is likened to a guard protecting the house. Ideally, the driveway should curve round to the side of the house to control the channelling of prosperous or malign forces entering or leaving.

A well-sited, well-aerated pool is a sign of good fortune and indicates the chance of a lucky windfall. The best position for a garden pond is outside the main entrance to a house, although it should not be too close to the front door as this may cause an accident, and may also allow excess yin to enter the house. If the pond is close to the building, a twisting or zigzag pathway leading to it will give an increased sense of distance. If you have a swimming pool it should be set back from the house because of the large amount of yin it holds, and it should also not be bigger than the house itself. The water in a pond or pool should always be kept clean in order to maintain a healthy flow of ch'i on the surface; decaying plants encourage sha to settle on the water, and this brings ill health and bad luck.

The same rule applies to drains and sewers. Drains should have a cover allowing water to filter through but preventing clogging from soil or dead leaves. Ch'i is also unbalanced by the influence of sewers, which can emit sha, and plant pots should be placed over them; this not only improves the visual appearance but also counteracts sha that may be rising from the sewer.

A driveway is one of the main ways that ch'i enters from the road into your garden. If your house or apartment is at or near the top of a hill, good fortune, and particularly money, could roll out of the house too quickly. A pool or a twisting driveway could help to slow this process down. Ideally the driveway should curve round to the side of the house, blocking direct access from the front door to the road. A light outside the house or in the driveway will encourage positive ch'i, which in turn will encourage a healthy life and prosperous career. The driveway should not be too narrow or too wide in proportion to the building. Ch'i has to squeeze down narrow entrances and floods rapidly into wide ones; your own ch'i and the ch'i of the house can either be drained or overcome by this flow. If there is sufficient room, a driveway should be wider at the entrance and taper as it approaches the house.

The Front Door

If you have a good feng shui reading for the position of your home and its surrounding area, it does not automatically mean you will obtain good feng shui readings within your home. Once ch'i has entered a building it has to deal with corridors, doors, windows, furniture and general household items. Ch'i circulates throughout the whole house, moving up and down stairs, from room to room, and under, above and around objects. Sometimes it is lost through windows or doors, but other times it is created by plants or flowers. Wherever it is and whatever it does, it is believed to affect our family relationships, our health and our sexuality, so its smooth passage throughout the home is of particular importance to our general well-being.

The positioning of the front or main door of the house is one of the most important features of any building since it is the major access point for ch'i, the point where lucky influences or destructive spirits can enter. It is also the protector of the house, as well as being the main thoroughfare between the home and the outside world. You can take a reading for the position of your front door using *The Feng Shui Kit* compass. However, unless you are building a house it is likely to be both difficult and expensive to change the position of this door if you have obtained an unlucky reading. If this is the case, the following guidelines will help you to improve the general feng shui of this important feature.

The front door should be upright, well-hinged and easy to open or close. If the door hinges rub or jam, or the door itself creaks and groans when it is used, the noise disturbs the harmony of the house as well as your own equilibrium. The door should be in proportion with the size of the house; a door that is too large dents the building and could cause financial problems, whereas a door that is too small could lead to family squabbles. The surrounding frame should also be straight and free of damp or dry rot. Further good ch'i can be ushered into the house by a light or lights attached to the outside wall or the side of the door, although a lamp-post should never stand directly outside the front door as it could obstruct the smooth flow of ch'i. Lamp-posts in the garden are likened to guards who keep watch over those who live in and enter the house. If you do have lights outside your house try to replace old bulbs immediately, especially if they are one of a pair, as they are a bad omen for the future.

A front door should open into a bright space to avoid the claustrophobic or oppressive feeling of entering a dark, cramped area. Ch'i needs room to breathe and move, and could easily be trapped in narrow lobbies or cramped conditions. If you have a small, airless lobby it can be improved by placing a mirror or light on the wall and a green-leafed plant in a corner. Draughts can also weaken ch'i inside the house, and cause poor health and bad temper, so make sure that there are no gaps or cracks at the side of or under the door.

Once you have opened the front door you may have to open an inner lobby door. This inner door can help to regulate the flow of ch'i, but be careful that too much ch'i does not rush into the house when opening doors that lead directly onto one another. Wind chimes above the doorway can calm ch'i, and traditionally they also frighten away any malign spirits trying to enter the house. If the front door opens straight into your living-room a screen could be placed near the door to avoid ch'i flooding in.

The front door of a house or apartment building should never face directly onto the corner of another house. It is said that the corner is like a dagger cutting into the home, and it will bring about financial loss and ill health. A building sited on the outside bend of a thoroughfare or river is also considered unlucky, since the route or river is compared to a blade slicing the house. In addition, locations near rivers are linked to arthritis and flu, which may arise as a result of damp air coming in from the river. A front door facing a dead

Wind chimes above or near a door are said to frighten away unlucky spirits and a light will encourage life-giving ch'i.

The feng shui reading for a small dark lobby can be improved by introducing a mirror or a large green-leafed plant.

A sharply curved road, bridge or railway line is likened to a knife slicing into property that faces its outside curve.

If the front door of your house faces a small gap between two buildings money could slip through your grasp.

The forces channelled down this long knife-like road are overwhelming for a house built at the end. A mirror at the entrance could dispel harmful influences.

The force of ch'i moving down the two paths of a Y-shaped road could be overwhelming and could adversely affect the health of those living opposite. The continual choice of direction could also cause confusion in the home.

end in the road will meet stagnant ch'i that has accumulated in corners; this could result in domestic arguments caused by moving through the sha which has gathered in this area. If your house is in an unfavourable position, pa kua or ordinary domestic mirrors will help to deflect unlucky influences.

Your front door should not be opposite a small gap between two buildings – such a gap is likened to a slice taken out of cake. Earnings or savings could slip through this space unless it is controlled by a fence, wall or line of trees. However, a barrier that protects you should be at least two metres away from the house, otherwise the ch'i will be ensnared in the small space created and the proximity of the wall will become overbearing. In some cases building and planning regulations may not allow for this amount of space, so if you do have a wall or fence close to the house place a mirror on the outside wall, allow ivy to grow up the fence or hang a blind on any window that faces it.

A front door facing onto a Y-shaped road or path is also an unlucky feng shui site. Ch'i coming down the two channels meets forcefully where the road joins and then moves towards the front door. This situation can create a state of confusion for those who live there; it is believed that when you continually face two directions it is hard to make a choice, and in turn this will affect work and family life.

Churches, monasteries, temples, funeral parlours and cemeteries are traditionally considered unlucky places to overlook. They are thought to be full of yin spirits and the refuge for ghosts, souls and the unknown, and for many they are a reminder of death. A bright light or wind chimes positioned outside the front door will frighten away lurking spirits, and blinds on any overlooking windows will give the building a certain protection. In the West there are many who are comfortable living near a religious building, although some feel a sense of unease at the idea of living close to a graveyard.

If you are living in a rural area observe the shape of the land behind and in front of your house. Your front door should not face a mountain or a hill, as the yang spirits are too powerful here and this could result in financial loss. Nor should the house be built on a steep hillside as the ch'i rolls down the hill too quickly; other houses, or a group of trees or bushes, at a higher level than your house could control the swift-moving ch'i. But if your house is built on a gentle slope with the front door overlooking a harbour or bay this is a fortunate site for both good financial fortune and personal well-being.

Interior Design

The guidelines outlined in the rest of this chapter will help you to maximize the potential for good feng shui when planning the interior design of your home. These guidelines should be combined with your own personal taste and preference, but you will also need to take into account the balance of yin and yang and the influence of colours on both the design of a room and on your own personality.

If you discover any unlucky directions in your home with your *Feng Shui Kit* compass, there are ways you can compensate for this through the colour scheme of a room and the objects it contains. For example, if your Pa Tzu element is fire you could decorate any areas where you have obtained a negative reading with colours and objects that are associated with an element that combines positively with fire. In this case both wood and earth combine well with fire so you could either choose a green colour scheme and introduce plants and wooden features or objects into the room, or a yellow colour scheme which incorporates earthy colours in paint and fabrics (*see page 44*).

You can also use the compass degrees on ring six of *The Feng Shui Kit* compass to help you with interior design. Make a note of the compass degrees every time you take a reading, and you will then immediately be able to identify your lucky and unlucky directions, and thus plan the design of your home accordingly.

The Main Bedroom

The main bedroom is one of the three most important rooms in a house, the other two being the kitchen and the living-room.

The feng shui of the main bedroom is of particular significance as it affects the domestic feng shui of the household, and the quality of sleep gained in this room is also influential on the relationships and health of those living in the house. It is possible to take a feng shui reading for the position of the bedroom by standing in the centre of the house and pointing the compass toward the direction of the room. To be more specific about the placing of the bed and furniture you can take a reading in the bedroom itself, directing the compass towards each item of furniture you want to assess.

In China, the head of the bed is usually placed towards the east, since the hottest side of the house is the western side. This tradition has carried through into feng shui and unless your compass reading specifies otherwise, this is considered the luckiest direction for the bed.

Sleepless nights are forecast when the head of the bed is positioned behind the bedroom door so that only the foot of the bed can be seen; you have no control over who or what enters the bedroom. Also, the bedroom door should not open directly onto the bed as this could drain away your energy. If you are unable to move the bed you could break the gap between the foot of the bed and the door by placing plants or a low chest of drawers or bookcase in this area. Make sure that the furniture around your bed is not too large or cumbersome as this could make you feel crowded and overwhelmed. From a practical point of view, the bed should not be placed opposite the mirror in case you wake up in the night and are suddenly frightened by your reflection. Ch'i should be able to circulate freely

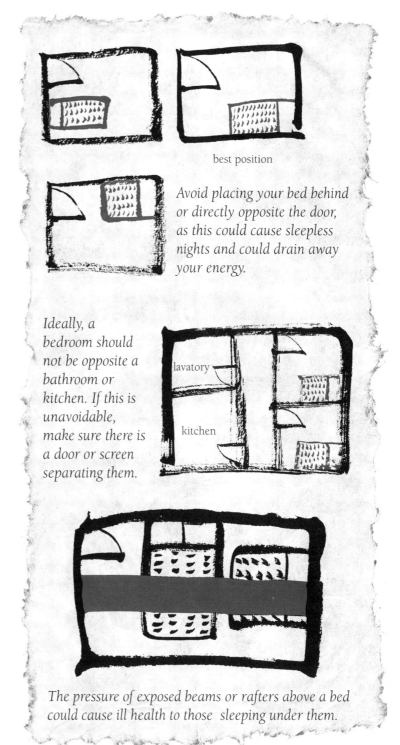

best position

Avoid placing your bed behind or directly opposite the door, as this could cause sleepless nights and could drain away your energy.

Ideally, a bedroom should not be opposite a bathroom or kitchen. If this is unavoidable, make sure there is a door or screen separating them.

lavatory

kitchen

The pressure of exposed beams or rafters above a bed could cause ill health to those sleeping under them.

Windows should not be larger than the front door unless they are divided into smaller panes of glass. The same rule applies to the individual windows and doors in relation to each room.

Windows with small panes of glass ensure that the ch'i coming through the door is not overwhelmed.

under the bed to avoid backache or damp, so you should make sure that there are wheels or legs on the bed to allow for this extra space.

Soft colours and gentle lighting encourage tranquillity in the bedroom whereas bright lights are believed to cause restlessness, especially if they are fitted to the wall above the bed. It is thought that very bright lights over the head of the bed could not only damage eyesight but also cause liver problems. If the bulbs in any of the bedroom lights should fail, remember to replace them with new ones immediately.

The bedroom should not directly face the kitchen or lavatory since the steam or smell can affect sleep, and the sha from blocked drains or rubbish bins can weaken healthy ch'i. If the bedroom is close to either of these rooms there should be a door or partition separating the two.

One of the unlucky feng shui signs affecting health is an exposed beam or rafter running across the centre of a room or above the bed. The beam is thought to carry the pressure of the house, as well as prevent the smooth passage of ch'i through a room. As exposed beams are believed to be oppressive, a bed should never be placed directly underneath one. A beam over the head of the bed may cause headaches and nervous disorders, over the middle of the bed it could result in

stomach disorders, and over the foot of the bed it could cause swelling of the feet. The most extreme remedy would be to install a false ceiling to cover any beams, but alternatively you could hang a mirror on the beam.

Windows with only one pane of glass should not be larger than the bedroom door otherwise the ch'i coming through the window becomes more powerful than the ch'i coming through the door. This rule does not apply if the windows have smaller panes. Ideally a window should open outwards to maximize the amount of ch'i that can enter, as a window that opens inwards can sometimes cut through the good ch'i inside a room.

The Kitchen

Chinese kitchens are traditionally associated with the eastern or south-eastern side of a house. The south is associated with the element of fire and the east with the element of wood; as wood was needed to produce fire these directions took on a symbolic significance. But practical reasoning also lies behind this choice. In China, the main door of the house traditionally faced south as the harsh winter weather came from the north. Since it was unlucky to have a kitchen facing directly onto the front door, cooking was usually done in the eastern side of the house, which was also open to south-easterly winds, used for igniting fuel.

RIGHT *The kitchen sink should not be next to the cooker as the two elements of water and fire do not combine well. Traditionally, the cooker should also be positioned away from any windows.*

The eastern and south-eastern sides of a house are traditionally regarded as the best position for the kitchen.

Make sure the fridge is not next to the cooker to avoid a clash between the elements of water and fire.

The kitchen, and especially the cooker, should not directly face the front or back door since positive ch'i will disappear quickly.

The rule of having a kitchen slightly to one side of the house still applies today, with the east and south-east being regarded as the luckiest directions. The kitchen is thought to be a 'treasure' as it is the place where those living in the house are fed and cared for, but if your kitchen door faces directly onto the front or back door of the house, the good ch'i that circulates there will disappear quickly. Also, the kitchen should not be opposite a lavatory door since germs may spread easily, and for the same reason the plumbing from the lavatory should not run under the kitchen floor. If your kitchen is unfavourably positioned you can install wall lights or introduce green-leafed plants to hold and stimulate positive ch'i. A mirror will deflect misfortune that may disturb the harmony of the kitchen.

The cooker is the focal point in a kitchen and should not be placed next to cold or wet areas as the two elements do not combine well: water extinguishes fire. In effect, the cooker should not sit next to the sink or the fridge, but if it does a piece of panelling should break contact between the two. It is also traditional to position the cooker away from any windows as the quality of food deteriorates when exposed to the sun, and any incoming wind might extinguish the cooking flame.

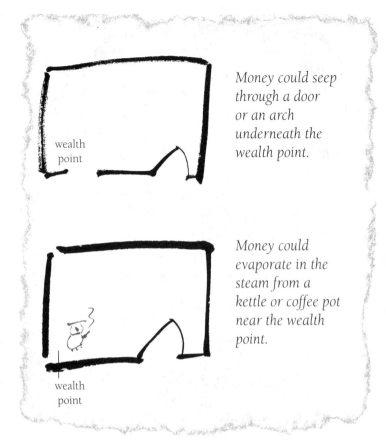

Money could seep through a door or an arch underneath the wealth point.

Money could evaporate in the steam from a kettle or coffee pot near the wealth point.

The Living-room

The living-room is a place where family or friends can meet and relax, and is best situated on the ground floor to provide easy access. The front door of a house can open directly into a living-room if the room is small, but if it is large there is a danger of too much ch'i entering or escaping, and a screen, piece of furniture or large plant should be positioned near the door to control the amount of ch'i flowing into or leaving the room.

As with other rooms in the house, the windows should not be too large unless they are divided into smaller panes, and ideally they should open outwards. Beams should either be hidden by a false ceiling or have a small mirror attached to them, and sharp corners, or edges that break the line of a wall, should be softened by a plant, painting or wall-hanging. Ch'i has to move around objects, so avoid cluttering your room, floor or surfaces with furniture or household items. If stairs lead down into the living-room, avoid placing a mirror at the foot of the stairs so that you do not stumble when you suddenly catch sight of your reflection. The only time a mirror should be placed in this position is when it is being used to counteract unlucky or malign influences, and even then it should only be a small ornamental mirror. Mirrors should, however, be placed near the foot of basement stairs to encourage yang into a yin area.

Positive ch'i can be encouraged into the room by introducing plants or water. An aquarium containing an odd number of goldfish invigorates ch'i, and adds a fresh, life-giving quality to the room. Goldfish are particularly popular as their colour is associated with wealth, and odd numbers are favoured as they are considered to be yang; water is yin so the two balance each other out. If your personal Pa Tzu element is water you should keep seven goldfish to counteract the yin of your element; all other feng shui elements need at least three goldfish to maintain a balance of yin and yang.

There is a point in the living-room known as the wealth point, and this can be found in the top left-hand corner as you enter the room. It is believed that a blockage in this area, or a door underneath it, can seriously affect your finances; if there is a kettle or coffee-maker here it is thought that the steam and heat will gradually draw your money away, or if there is a door your money will slip through it. It is a good idea to introduce plants which encourage financial prosperity – these have large, rounded green leaves, and any dead shoots or leaves should be removed immediately in order to maintain a life-giving and productive air. The larger your plant and plant pot, the greater the chance of good fortune. Further good forces can be gathered by placing three coins wrapped in red paper under the pot. The coins symbolize wealth and the colour red denotes prosperity and good fortune (see below).

Colours

You can find the colour associated with your personal Pa Tzu element listed in chapter three (see page 44), and the characteristics associated with the five elemental colours are listed below. Generally, the home needs a variety of colour to create a sense of harmony, and you will have to use your own intuition to gauge this balance in relation to the furnishings in the home, and those who live there.

Red

Red is considered to be one of the luckiest colours and is associated with good fortune, prosperity and strength. Small packets of lucky red money are given to children at Chinese new year, blessings are usually written on red and gold paper, and red-dyed eggs are traditionally presented to new-born children.

Green

Green is associated with tranquillity and freshness. It is also the colour of spring and is a sign of new life. It is believed that dreams will end happily if they feature shades of green. The combination of red and green is thought to be both fortunate and influential.

Yellow

Yellow was the imperial colour of China. From the sixth century onwards, yellow was the accepted colour for the emperor and ordinary citizens were not permitted to wear yellow clothes (with the exception of Buddhist monks). Yellow is also associated with fame, progress and advancement, and is closely linked with the earth, as fertile earth in some areas of China has a yellow hue.

Black

Black is associated with honour, although it can also indicate darkness or herald unfortunate events. In Chinese theatre, the appearance of eight heroes with blackened faces is a sign of honourable men. Black was also the colour worn by the first emperor of China after he defeated the Chou dynasty, who wore the colour red; he chose black as it is associated with the element water, and water extinguishes fire, represented by the colour red.

White

White is the colour of autumn and the sign of old age. Although it is said to be the colour of mourning, traditionally unbleached sackcloth would be worn for this purpose, and this was more yellow-brown in colour. Pure white is associated with purity and virginity.

CHAPTER FIVE

FENG SHUI AT WORK

Wealth

Your performance at work or the success of your business is determined by site and arrangement as much as by the efficiency of the company or the standard of service it provides. For many who believe strongly in feng shui, even an ideally located business offering excellent service cannot prosper if the layout of the building encourages bad ch'i. Although many of the feng shui rules of the home also apply to business, there is an extra feng shui dimension believed to encourage a healthy flow of money.

You can combine a personal reading from *The Feng Shui Kit* compass with the advice below to improve the feng shui of your work environment. If you discover that one of the following guidelines clashes with your individual compass reading you should use a direction which does give you a lucky reading. When arranging furniture in an office it is also a good idea to use your *Feng Shui Kit* ruler to determine whether the height of desks, tables or cash registers, for example, matches the categories of prosperity, career, growth or wealth.

A Prosperous Site

If you are planning to start a business choose a site in an already flourishing business district; this indicates

A business with an entrance facing a narrow gap between two buildings runs the risk of losing its profits through the gap.

If the entrance faces the corner of another building, this is likened to a knife cutting into the business and slicing through the profits.

that successful ch'i is flowing through that area. Your office should not be dwarfed by the surrounding buildings, as your good fortune will be overpowered and ch'i will not be able to flow smoothly in and around the building. If the buildings on the Green Dragon side are higher than your building this will not have any detrimental effects on your business, as the Green Dragon has an active spirit. If the buildings on the White Tiger side are higher you should build a roof garden or pool to stimulate the ch'i of the smaller building. If the buildings opposite the main entrance are higher you should attempt to raise the height of the building by erecting signs above roof level. You could also place wooden, metal or stone shapes that symbolize swords on the roof; these act like knives cutting into the bad fortune that descends from taller buildings.

If all the surrounding buildings are taller you can combine the above-mentioned methods as well as placing mirrors on the outside walls to deflect the unlucky or overpowering influences.

For structural reasons, and in the interest of good health, the building should not be on low-lying land or near waste disposal areas. The appearance of the building also affects its prosperity; the entrance to the premises should be above street level, windows and doors should be in good repair, and paths should be cleared of any weeds and rubbish. If the entrance is at street level you should build a small step and increase the height of the floor level inside, even if it is only by a few inches.

The front door should not face a fork in the road as this results in good fortune being misdirected, and debts could build up. It is also unlucky if the entrance is opposite a narrow gap between two buildings, as this gap could drain away the profits of the business. If corners of other buildings face the front door, these are likened to knives cutting into your business, slowly slicing through your profits; to remedy this situation you can position a mirror to ward off the cutting effect of a corner, and place a screen at the entrance to your

A mountain or hill facing the main entrance is overpowering and impedes the flow of ch'i leaving the building.

The outside bend of a road, bridge or flyover is like a scythe cutting away at the good fortune of the business.

The land at the back of the building should not slope downhill as the good business ch'i will roll away too quickly.

A business protected by the 'jade belt' is likely to be successful.

An ideal position for a work place in a rural area. The building is protected by a hill at the back, and the main entrance overlooks the sea allowing the positive forces to flow through the front entrance first.

An office entrance should not face the end of a cul-de-sac as trapped malign spirits exert an unfavourable influence on the surrounding area.

Exposed drains and pipes on the front of a building draw money away from the business.

building so that access is moved slightly to one side, blocking the bad fortune. Although water is generally associated with money, a fast moving stream or river outside the entrance could drain away success.

The shape of the land at the back and the front of the site is also influential. If you work in a rural area, a hill or mountain facing the entrance is overpowering, and forms an obstacle to the flow of ch'i leaving the building – a screen made of wood or stone, or a line of trees near the front door will help the ch'i to flow smoothly. The land in front should be flat or, preferably, sloping slightly downhill, and the land at the back slightly higher. The back door should not face the sea or a valley as the positive forces from these features need to flow through the front door first; a barrier made of wood outside the back door will discourage these positive forces from entering the building through this access point.

The front door of your work place should not face a cemetery or any religious buildings, since they are believed to be full of restless spirits which are yin in nature and disturb the yin/yang balance. There is a tradition of hanging wind chimes to frighten away wandering spirits; those who believe strongly in the power of feng shui may even board up the entrance and build a new one on a different side of the building. The restless spirits do not, however, disturb businesses that deal with religious artefacts or issues.

The outside bend of a curved road, bridge or flyover is said to be like a scythe cutting away at your good fortune, but a work place that nestles inside a curve is protected by what is referred to as the 'jade belt'. (Jade belts were worn by Chinese nobility, and jade is associated with immortality and purity.) Drains and pipes that are attached to the front of the building should be covered as they syphon money away from the business. Any major water pipes should be at the back of the building so that rain-water can be channelled away from the front. It is also unlucky if the entrance to your

White Tiger · Green Dragon

LEFT *The front door should be on the side of the Green Dragon, as this symbolizes activity. Although the White Tiger is usually quiet, it can sometimes disrupt the efficiency of a business.*

RIGHT *If the main entrance to a work place stretches across the front of the building, the main access point should still be on the side of the Green Dragon.*

White Tiger · Green Dragon

The front door should not open directly onto a staircase as good ch'i can easily escape into the street through a door in continual use.

The kitchen should not be visible from the main entrance unless the business is connected with catering, otherwise the noise and activity may prove overwhelming to customers.

The front door should not face a lavatory as the yin spirits may clash with the yang spirits entering the building.

office faces the end of a cul-de-sac: malign spirits become trapped here and exert an unfavourable influence on the surrounding area. A well-placed mirror or wind chimes can help to deflect this bad fortune.

As with the home, the main door of the building is the major entrance for ch'i, but since work is closely linked to the outside world the entrance should be higher and wider than a domestic front door. A wide and well-decorated entrance is also welcoming; not only does it draw in passers-by but it also encourages good business ch'i to enter. The customer should not feel trapped by limited space once they are through the door – the pressure created by a confined space on first entering does not produce a positive atmosphere and this could carry through into any negotiations. Also, inner doors should be smaller than the front door to avoid them overwhelming the incoming energy. It is said that the spirit of prosperity that comes from a shop draws customers to it even if they are not sure whether it stocks the goods that they need or want.

The front door should be built on the side of the Green Dragon, the right-hand side as you face the building. If the entrance stretches the full length of the building the main access point should still be on the right-hand side, as the Green Dragon symbolizes activity. The White Tiger, on the left-hand side of the building, is usually quiet, but when disturbed it can rise in anger and disrupt the efficiency of the business.

A front door should never face directly onto a staircase as this is the channel by which ch'i circulates through a building. If the front door is continually opened and closed, good ch'i could easily slip away into the street. This rule also applies to the lavatory as it is a source of strong yin spirits, and these could clash with the yang spirits entering the building. In addition, unless the building is connected with catering, the kitchen should not be visible from the front door; the activity, noise and steam that comes from a kitchen is overwhelming to customers at first sight.

Inside the Work Place

The most vibrant parts of the work place are the director's office and the accounts office. Unlucky feng shui in either of these areas affects the morale and success of the whole business. Bad feng shui in other areas weakens a 'limb' of the business, but unlucky feng shui at the top weakens the whole of the 'body'.

Access to the director's office should be bright and spacious so that ch'i can enter evenly and flow freely. Offices at the end of long, dark corridors trap the ch'i and weaken managerial control. Offices that lead off corridors are acceptable as long as the corridors are well lit and access is clear. If the offices are in the same building as residential accommodation there should be separate lavatories for the two areas. The director's office should be on a higher floor or at a higher level than the lavatory so that sha cannot enter the office if there are any blockages or problems with the drains.

The position of desks within an office is very important in determining the efficiency of the staff, and is especially important for the director of a company. Unless your business is reliant on customers entering a shop, the director's desk should never be in the public eye as privacy and peace are needed for maximum concentration. If there are other desks in the director's office they should be placed in orderly rows around the main desk to allow for an even flow of ch'i around the furniture. A door should never open directly onto a desk, but to avoid the element of surprise anyone working at a desk should be able to see who is coming into the office; in some cases it may be necessary to install a mirror for this purpose.

The best position for a desk is in a corner opposite the door with your back to the wall, and you can further increase the flow of good ch'i by placing plants or lights behind the desk. A wall creates a feeling of stability and is likened to a mountain offering support and protection, lights encourage more ch'i into the room, and plants add new ch'i as well as enliven sluggish ch'i.

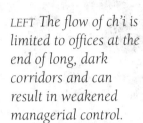

LEFT *The flow of ch'i is limited to offices at the end of long, dark corridors and can result in weakened managerial control.*

RIGHT *In a shared office, the director's desk should be in the luckiest position, with other desks arranged in neat rows to allow for the smooth flow of ch'i around the furniture.*

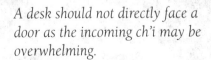

A desk should not directly face a door as the incoming ch'i may be overwhelming.

The element of surprise is strong if you sit with your back to the door. A mirror should be installed above the desk to enable you to see who is coming in.

The best position for a desk is in the far corner opposite the door so you are sitting with your back to the wall. The wall creates a feeling of stability, and plants and lamps on or around the desk attract good ch'i and improve its flow.

If you sit with your back to a door or close to a window your concentration and authority is said to slip through the 'empty door'. Generally, appropriately placed mirrors, desk lamps and plants can help to remedy the effects of a badly positioned desk.

This ideal positioning for desks also applies to safes and cash registers. If your business is not dependent on contact with the public, accounts should be calculated in a quiet, concealed place, but if you work in a shop or a restaurant the cash register should be at the heart of the business to encourage money into the shop.

Plants, aquariums, paintings, prints and certain colours are also believed to add to the prosperity of a business. Fish are thought to denote money, since the Chinese word for fish (*yu*) sounds similar to that for excess (*yu*). As in the home, an odd number of goldfish in an aquarium are believed to be lucky: in the work place they are thought to attract money, and if bubbles are added through a water filter, fresh ch'i is also increased. Plants and shrubs activate ch'i and illustrations of landscapes or plants create harmony. If you have calculated your Pa Tzu compass at the beginning of the book and your trigram is Li or Chen you should surround yourself with large green-leaved plants, but if your trigram is Ken or K'un you should control the level of greenery – a plant at the door or the wealth point will be sufficient. All other trigrams are suited to a balanced amount of greenery. This advice applies to the home as well as the work place: the wealth point in a house or apartment is in the living-room, and in a work place it is usually in a quiet, private room where important financial decisions are made.

Colour

The use of colour varies according to the type of business. Red and gold are traditionally associated with good fortune and are often the colours used to decorate Chinese restaurants or shops. Businesses that deal with trade should have vases of flowers with large blooms, such as peonies or lilies; if this is not possible, illustrations of flowers should be displayed instead. Basic black and white designs are appropriate for military or police offices, while a brighter and less regulated use of colour is suitable for media or advertising environments. Whatever colours, plants or illustrations are used, they should create a sense of balance since they affect the nature of those in the room as well as the movement of ch'i.

CHAPTER SIX

RURAL FENG SHUI

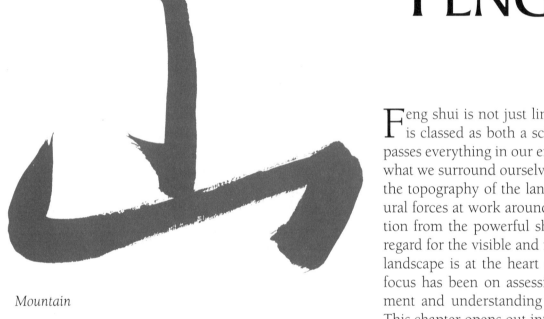

Mountain

Feng shui is not just limited to an object or place: it is classed as both a science and an art that encompasses everything in our environment. How we live and what we surround ourselves with is intricately linked to the topography of the land, and the elements and natural forces at work around us; we do not exist in isolation from the powerful shaping effects of nature. This regard for the visible and invisible forces at work in the landscape is at the heart of feng shui. Up to now, the focus has been on assessing your immediate environment and understanding feng shui in an urban area. This chapter opens out into the wider area of rural feng shui and introduces the principles that are influential on our surroundings.

The symbols and language of feng shui have been inspired by the splendour of the Chinese landscape, in particular its mountains and rivers; it is their interaction that produces the endless shapes and patterns of the land. Mountains and hills control the flow of water, and in return water nourishes the earth. You can determine rich points of ch'i by an abundance of thriving vegetation in the landscape, whereas stunted plant growth and arid landscapes indicate areas that are starved of healthy ch'i. The shapes of every mountain and watercourse are significant, as is the fertility of the land, the amount of sunlight or shadow, the position of existing buildings, and the overall atmosphere that is created by these various elements. Thus the ability to determine both favourable and unfavourable natural features in the landscape is invaluable when choosing a place to settle, as well as helping those who already live in a rural area to determine the fortune of their home.

The Tao and Nature

Tao is the Whole,
The Whole contains the Universe.
The Universe contains the Earth.
The Earth contains Humankind.
These are the four great elements of creation.

(*Tao Te Ching*, Timothy Freke and Martin Palmer)

The idea of living in harmony with the Tao, the way of nature, has been at the heart of Chinese philosophy for over two-and-a-half thousand years. The Tao is in everything, and gives the universe its order, unity and rhythm. This philosophy gave the Chinese an inherent respect for nature, which is why their temples, farms and houses were designed to enhance the landscape not detract from it. The buildings themselves were traditionally built from local resources, such as stone, plant fibre and wood, and in many rural areas they still are today. The whole rural scene is a reflection of the relationship between the three main forces of the universe: heaven, earth and humanity.

In Chinese religion heaven was, and still is, regarded as the most powerful force in the universe, inhabited by gods, goddesses, spirits and wise sages known as the Immortals; the Jade Emperor ruled over them all. The emperor of China, regarded as the son of heaven and given a mandate to rule by heaven, provided the link between humans and heaven. The bond between humans and the earth was also powerful since China was largely an agrarian economy. The year was calculated according to the changes of the moon, the cycle of seasons, and the planting and harvesting of crops. At the beginning of each agricultural year the emperor would initiate and lead religious rituals to re-establish harmony throughout the country and seek auspicious blessings for the coming year. Through these rituals the emperor, as the symbol of humanity, consolidated the relationship between heaven, earth and humanity.

Even though the age of emperors has long passed, and for millions the rural life has been replaced by an urban one, the notion of a human bond with the natural world is still maintained in feng shui. A feng shui expert can read the landscape and identify strengths and weaknesses in natural formations, and is also aware of our limitations in relation to the natural elements, forces and features.

Mountains and hills

One of the favourite subjects of Chinese landscape painters is mountainous landscape. The mountain has always been regarded as the point at which heaven and earth meet. It is the abode of hermits, a place of pilgrimage and sacrifice, and its slopes are dotted with temples and shrines. Towering mist-shrouded peaks and pinnacles give way to hills, waterfalls, and groves of trees, and they in their turn ease into plains and rivers. People are dotted across the landscape, sailing along rivers, ploughing fields and living on mountainsides; they thus become subordinate to the power of the natural features. This idea of living in harmony with the natural order is a reflection of the Tao.

The mountain peaks in a classic Chinese landscape tower towards heaven, but their steepness and sharpness is offset by the lower foothills and plains that stretch below the peaks. Without foothills or gently undulating land as a counterbalance, the yang of the mountain peaks would not be balanced out. In contrast, clouds are yin and low-lying plains produce yin, and need the yang of the peaks to create a dynamic

A classic Chinese landscape. The yang of the mountain peaks is counterbalanced by the yin of the low-lying plain and the clouds to create a dynamic harmony.

harmony. Thus the least promising rural feng shui site is a flat, featureless plain; there are few trees, shrubs, plants or streams to produce ch'i and no hills, valleys or towns to channel it or slow it down.

Any land, whether mountainous or featureless, is still home to the dragon, the mythical creature that runs across the land with ch'i pulsing through its body. The dragon's body is always found in a linear formation tracing the lines of hills or marks along the ground. The watercourses flowing through the land are the ducts of the dragon, and since water is everywhere the dragon is also everywhere. In the tradition of feng shui the land, in all formations, is the earth dragon, and rivers and streams are the water dragon.

The dragon is the most powerful creature believed to be lying across the land and is central to traditional feng shui, but it is not the only creature seen in the shapes and forms of the land. In a sense, the shapes of the land can be what you want them to be; their forms are reminiscent of people, animals or objects, and they take on the character of that association. Sometimes, when bad luck or good fortune has struck a certain area, those who are affected look at the landscape and try to discern a feature that may be influencing their fortune. A hill or rock may look like the claws of a tiger, a house without a roof, an upturned boat, an open book or an offering bowl. This association can go some way to explaining a continued run of bad luck or, conversely, a streak of good fortune. For example, if a feature of the landscape is linked with a continual run of bad luck, remedies can usually be found. Stones or earth may be added to alter the shape, and a wall could be built, trees planted, or a shrine or pagoda erected to bring harmony into the landscape. Similarly, when a feature linked with good luck is harmed, perhaps as a result of building work or road construction, efforts should be made to counteract the damage to the site.

Particular shapes of boulders, hills and mountains are linked to the five elements of wood, metal, fire,

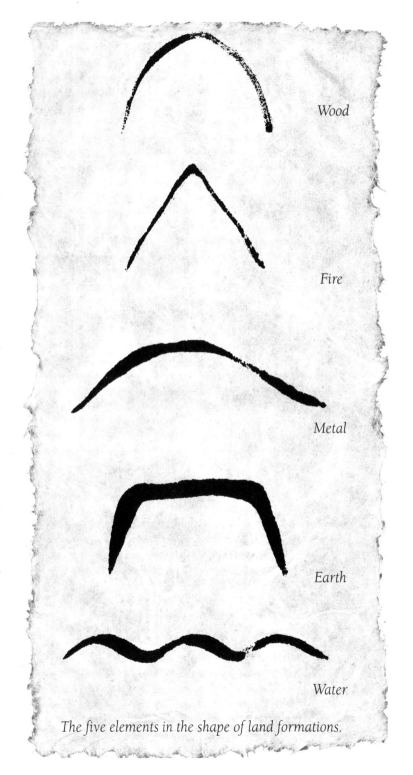

Wood

Fire

Metal

Earth

Water

The five elements in the shape of land formations.

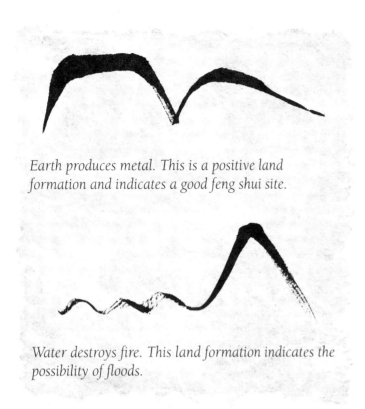

Earth produces metal. This is a positive land formation and indicates a good feng shui site.

Water destroys fire. This land formation indicates the possibility of floods.

earth and water. When certain elemental shapes are interpreted in the land they can be productive or destructive depending on the wider feng shui reading for that area. For example, a family who have a thriving timber business may attribute part of their success to nearby boulders or hills that are shaped like the element wood, whereas a business that has plumbing problems, or has suffered floods, may look to water-shaped hills as the root of the problem. Lucky and unlucky omens can be found according to need and circumstance.

Towards the end of the nineteenth century, Hong Kong was constantly plagued by outbreaks of fire. This was attributed to the shape of the foothill at the base of the peak of Hong Kong Island. The foothill had the shape of the element fire and the main peak resembled a wood pile; as a result the fire continually ignited the wood from below.

Trees

Healthy trees are a sign of healthy ch'i in the earth. The more fruitful and verdant the tree, the more likely it is to bring good fortune to that site. Trees can be the guardians of a site, protecting it from malign influences and producing life-giving ch'i. But a scarred or dying tree can have the opposite effect, draining the site of energy or life-breath. You should take care of the bushes and trees in your surrounding area by cutting back any dead branches, and either treating or removing dying trees, so as to encourage good fortune to your home. If you are thinking of planting new trees, evergreens are regarded as especially lucky as their leaves continually produce ch'i, and often one well-placed evergreen tree creates a better feng shui area than a whole row of trees.

Water

Great goodness is like water,
It flows everywhere, filling everything.
It is life-giving, by its very nature.
It humbly settles in the lowest places,
Like someone who follows Tao.

(*Tao Te Ching*, Timothy Freke and Martin Palmer)

An ideal site in relation to a watercourse is embraced by a river or stream that gently meanders, so allowing life-giving ch'i to flow smoothly along its course. A building positioned in the soft curves or folds of a watercourse is affected by this well-balanced ch'i. In contrast, sharp bends in a stream, or an abrupt end to its course, form arrow-like lines that not only break the flow of ch'i but also provide a channel for sha or malign forces which encourage bad fortune to the site.

If you do live in a fortunate location, the smooth flow of ch'i along the watercourse surrounding your house will encourage prosperity and good health into your home. However, there are also a number of unfavourable locations which may bring bad luck and

Favourable locations in relation to a watercourse.

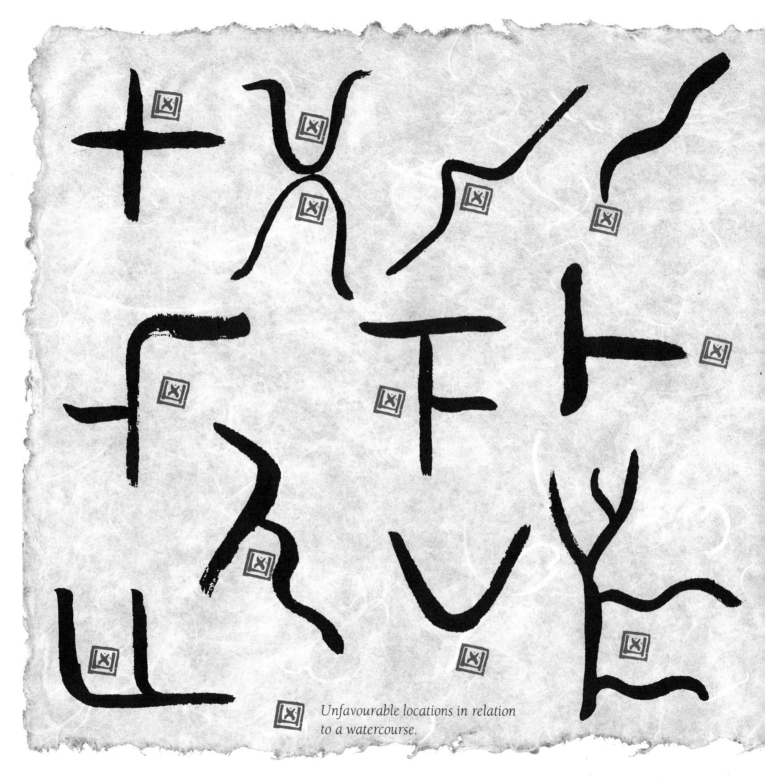

Unfavourable locations in relation to a watercourse.

ill health into your home. If you live on one of these sites there are ways you can compensate for this unfortunate positioning, and deter the malign influence of sha from entering your home. Well-positioned mirrors can be used to deflect malign forces, and healthy plants and foliage will encourage ch'i to the site, and also form a protective screen.

The five elements are not only seen in the varying forms of mountains and hills, but are also linked to certain shapes in rivers or streams. According to the 'Water Dragon Classic', water, earth and metal are regarded as the luckiest formations (there are two possible shapes for earth). As with land formations, when rivers or streams of different elemental shapes meet it can be either a productive or destructive combination; the outcome depends on the relationship of the elements. You can refer back to the table in chapter three to check

Metal

Earth

Wood

Fire

Water

The five elements in the shape of watercourses.

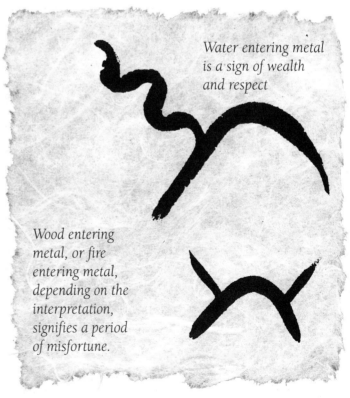

Water entering metal is a sign of wealth and respect

Wood entering metal, or fire entering metal, depending on the interpretation, signifies a period of misfortune.

these combinations (*see page 44*). For example, wood entering metal, or fire entering metal, depending on how you interpret the shapes, denotes a period of family misfortune, whereas water entering metal is a sign of wealth and respect.

Feng Shui and the Environment

Whether you are planning to buy or build a house in a rural or urban area, the same underlying rules apply. There may be rivers, valleys and hills instead of high-rise buildings, roads and shopping centres, but you should still be able to sense the flow and dispersal of ch'i and the interaction of yin and yang. Perhaps the hills are too high, exposed or overpowering? Or maybe the river bends are too sharp, or do not meander gently so creating a sense of peace? Always be aware of your surroundings; look for ways to improve the dynamic harmony of the area in which you live.

You need to make sure that trees, plants and shrubs are healthy, not withered or stunted, or you may need to plant trees, shrubs or crops in areas which have been stripped of vegetation. Make use of the natural resources around you, such as stone and timber, to help create a sense of balance in relation to the local landscape. You may find that there are a number of ways you could make the architecture or colour of your home harmonize with the colours and shapes of its surroundings.

It is not always possible to create a perfect site. There is the threat of pollution in the air and water, and also on the land, and inevitably the growing demand for housing comes into conflict with the need to preserve natural features. In rural areas there may be a legacy of mining, quarrying or deforestation that is hard to repair. Often, small scale activity at grass roots level can begin to rectify damage to the land, air or water.

At a practical level, feng shui requires a sensitivity to both the urban and rural environment. In this respect, the sensible practice of feng shui is akin to sound environmental planning; attempts can be made to rectify the past and efforts made to shape your immediate and future environment.

AFTERWORD

The information in this book is a guide to the art of feng shui, but since every situation and individual need is different, every reading will be different. Feng shui experts have their own personal methods of divination and there are no hard and fast rules to define the practice.

Feng shui was originally a practical science. The feng shui master assessed sites, offered advice and suggested change, but he was neither a priest nor a magician. He understood the subtleties of yin and yang and the movement of ch'i but he did not make astrological forecasts, create charms or act as an intermediary with a spirit world. These were additions that developed over the centuries, and there are still experts who are versed in these skills today.

Without years of training, the ordinary person cannot function at the same level as a master. However, much of feng shui is common sense fused with a particular Chinese understanding of nature. It is not always possible to create an ideal house or garden or identify the perfect site; imperfections and problems are to be expected, but do not be put off by an unfortunate reading. There is always the possibility for correction, change and improvement in every situation.

This book offers a window into a Chinese world view. Feng shui can be practised by anyone at any level – what you bring is your own character, intuition and common sense.

BIBLIOGRAPHY

Theodore de Bary (ed.), *T'ai-chi-t'u Shou, Sources of Chinese Tradition, Vol. 1.* Columbia University Press, 1960

Wolfram Eberhard, *A Dictionary of Chinese Symbols.* New York: Routledge Kegan Paul, 1986

Stephen D.R. Feuchtwang, *An Anthropological Analysis of Chinese Geomancy.* Taipei: Southern Materials Center Inc., 1974

Timothy Freke and Martin Palmer, *Tao Te Ching.* London: Piatkus, 1995

Man-Ho Kwok (trans.), Joanne O'Brien (ed.), *Chinese Myths and Legends.* London: Arrow, 1990

Man-Ho Kwok, Joanne O'Brien, *The Elements of Feng Shui.* Dorset, England: Element Books 1991

Man-Ho Kwok with Martin Palmer and Joanne O'Brien, *Authentic Chinese Horoscopes.* London: Arrow 1987

D. C. Lau (trans.), *Mencius.* London: Penguin, 1960

Evelyn Lip, *Chinese Geomancy.* Singapore: Times Books International, 1979

Joseph Needham, *Science and Civilisation in China, History of Scientific Thought, Vol. 2.* Cambridge University Press, 1956

Martin Palmer, Man-Ho Kwok, Joanne O'Brien, *The Fortune Teller's I Ching.* London: Century, 1986.

Martin Palmer (translated from the original Chinese), *The Shih Ching,* a collection of ancient Chinese poems. Available in English as *The She King,* James Legge (trans.), from *The Chinese Classics Vol. IV,* Oxford University Press, 1971; reprinted by Southern Materials Center Inc., Taipei, 1983.

Martin Palmer (ed.), *T'ung Shu, The Ancient Chinese Almanac.* London: Rider, 1986

Sarah Rossbach, *Feng Shui.* London: Rider, 1984

INDEX OF CHINESE TERMS

The Wade-Giles romanization, the most familiar and widely used system for transliterating Chinese into European languages, has been used in the text of this book. Since in 1958 Hanyu Pinyin was adopted as the official system of transliteration of the People's Republic of China, we have included a table giving the Hanyu Pinyin equivalents to all the Chinese terms that have been used in this book, and also giving the Chinese characters for each term (*see opposite*).

For ease of reference, the Chinese characters for each of the sixty-four hexagrams have also been included along with each interpretation in the text, as there are a number of terms with identical spelling but different characters.

INDEX

Page numbers in *italics* refer to illustrations

ACKNOWLEDGEMENTS

We would like to thank our colleagues and friends at ICOREC, Martin Palmer, Elizabeth Breuilly, Josephine Edwards and Stephen Robinson for their invaluable support and advice during the preparation of this book. We would also like to express our gratitude to our editor Tessa Monina, art editor Sarah Howerd, and illustrator Meilo So.

EDDISON·SADD EDITIONS

Editor	Tessa Monina
Proofreader	Pat Pierce
Indexer	Sue Martin
Creative Director	Nick Eddison
Art Director	Elaine Partington
Art Editor	Sarah Howerd
Illustrator	Meilo So
Production	Hazel Kirkman and Charles James